HTML
STYLE SHEETS

Quick Reference

HTML
STYLE SHEETS
Quick Reference

Rob Falla

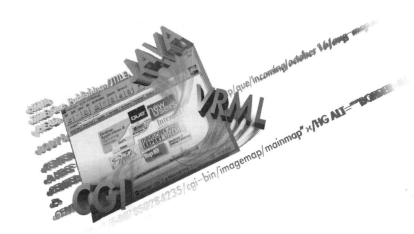

HTML Style Sheets Quick Reference

Copyright© 1997 by Que® Corporation.

Credits

President
Roland Elgey

Publisher
Joseph B. Wikert

Publishing Manager
Jim Minatel

Title Manager
Mark Cierzniak

Editorial Services Director
Elizabeth Keaffaber

Managing Editor
Sandy Doell

Director of Marketing
Lynn E. Zingraf

Acquisitions Editor
Stephanie Gould

Production Director
Jon Steever

Production Editor
William F. McManus

Editor
Sean Dixon

Product Marketing Manager
Kim Margolius

Assistant Product Marketing Manager
Christy M. Miller

Strategic Marketing Manager
Barry Pruett

Technical Editors
Ernie Sanders
Tony Wasson

Technical Support Specialist
Nadeem Muhammed

Acquisitions Coordinator
Jane K. Brownlow

Software Relations Coordinator
Patty Brooks

Book and Cover Designer
Nathan Clement

Production Team
Marcia Brizendine
DiMonique Ford
Amy Gornik
Dan Julian
Paul Wilson

Indexer
Nadia Ibrahim

Composed in Frutiger and ITC Kabel by Que Corporation.

For Kathy, my loving wife

For James Seraphin Sr.

About the Author

Rob Falla is a computer author, professional Web developer, freelance writer, and speculative fiction writer. He recently won first place for a speculative fiction short story titled "The October Comet." Rob is currently living in Nanticoke, Ontario, with his wife Kathy and their two daughters. Rob is available for any questions or comments through e-mail at **rfalla@cwebdev.com**.

Acknowledgements

The following people deserve to be singled out for the incredible effort they put into this book and the patience they all displayed during the various stages of this project. They were all there to answer questions, dig up software, and provide support when needed.

Kathy Falla—my loving wife and companion who was there for me

Mark Cierzniak—Title Manager

Stephanie Gould—Acquisitions Editor

Jon Steever—Product Development Specialist

Bill McManus—Production Editor

Thanks also to the rest of the support staff at Que.

This book was written as a team effort. Every member of the team helped out in a very important way. So, thanks team.

Rob

We'd Like to Hear from You!

As part of our continuing effort to produce books of the highest possible quality, Que would like to hear your comments. To stay competitive, we *really* want you, as a computer book reader and user, to let us know what you like or dislike most about this book or other Que products.

You can mail comments, ideas, or suggestions for improving future editions to the address below, or send us a fax at (317) 581-4663. For the online inclined, Macmillan Computer Publishing has a forum on CompuServe (type **GO QUEBOOKS** at any prompt) through which our staff and authors are available for questions and comments. The address of our Internet site is **http://www.mcp.com** (World Wide Web).

In addition to exploring our forum, please feel free to contact me personally to discuss your opinions of this book: I'm **jsteever@que. mcp.com** on the Internet.

Thanks in advance—your comments will help us to continue publishing the best books available on computer topics in today's market.

Jon Steever
Product Development Specialist
Que Corporation
201 W. 103rd Street
Indianapolis, Indiana 46290
USA

Contents at a Glance

Table of Contents

HTML Style Sheets Quick Reference

Contents

HTML Style Sheets Quick Reference

Contents

WELCOME TO QUE'S HTML STYLE SHEETS QUICK REFERENCE!

The World Wide Web is constantly evolving and changing. It is for this reason that new ways must be found to better present the content of the Web. HTML style sheets mark a new beginning in Web design and development.

Compatibility issues have plagued HTML authors since the day a second browser was released to the Internet community because not all browsers render the same HTML tags, and no browser renders them all. There has always been a noticeable difference in the appearance of Web pages, depending on the browser being used to display the Web pages.

With the long awaited release of cascading style sheets (CSS), many—if not all—of these layout differences will finally be resolved. Through the use of just one style sheet, a Web page author can achieve a consistent appearance on one, five, or hundreds of Web pages—when using a CSS compliant browser.

Que's *HTML Style Sheets Quick Reference* will help you implement style sheets into your next Web site. Each CSS element is described in its own entry, along with additional background regarding some of its most important attributes.

HTML 3 is the minimum language requirement for style sheets. In most cases, though, this minimum requirement will not be sufficient. Internet Explorer has already released a CSS-compliant browser (MSIE 3.0.02). Netscape Navigator 4 apparently will also support CSS1, the cascading style sheets standard.

QUICK TABLES

There are two distinct ways to use reference material. Those who are new to the subject will make use of the table of contents to locate a general topic for their starting point. People already familiar with the subject will skip the table of contents, relying instead on the index.

With these two distinct styles in mind, this book is designed with jump tables and quick tables. Jump tables direct you to the more specific quick tables. Quick tables allow the reader to quickly locate a topic-specific starting point—like an index—by page number.

How to Use Quick Tables

The "Building Cascading Style Sheets" jump table leads you to category-specific quick tables. You can quickly find the category you want and look up the more detailed quick table for that category.

Many people discover that linking between tables (and the elements to which they point) is an effective way to minimize look-up time.

Building Cascading Style Sheets

You can use this jump table as a starting point for developing cascading style sheets. Find a category of interest and jump to the corresponding table. That table will lead you to more specific information, allowing you to narrow the category even further.

Basic Concepts of Cascading Style Sheets

The following table will lead you step-by-step through the process of designing cascading style sheets, including usage of the various attributes. Refer to the quick table on this page.

Pseudo-Classes and Pseudo-Elements

For first-time CSS users, I recommend that you follow this table—topic by topic—to understand the basic concepts of HTML. Once you have completed this section, you should be able to rely on the remaining tables as quick references while developing your style sheets.

Pseudo-Classes and Pseudo-Elements

Cascading style sheets allow for pseudo-classes and pseudo-elements, which cover areas not addressed in the standard CSS model. The pseudo-classes and pseudo-elements enable CSS to accept external information that influences the formatting process.

The Cascade

The cascade, simply put, is the order of operations for the style sheet. The style sheet implementations are given certain weight over the influence of the presentation based on their position in the HTML document.

To learn more about...	Go to page...
Cascading Order	46

Formatting Model

This table includes proper formatting techniques for CSS, such as margins, borders, padding, and so on. Additionally, it demonstrates how features can be inherited.

To learn more about...	Go to page...
Vertical Formatting	170
Horizontal Formatting	83
Lists	100
Floating Elements	68

CSS1 Properties

The defined style properties of CSS1 are presented in the following table. You can use this table to find the style property you want to use. Look up a style for a list of values associated with that property.

Be creative! Have fun! CSS gives you the design control you previously could only dream about when using plain HTML. USE IT!

To learn more about...	Go to page...
Font Properties	73
Font Encoding	69-79
Color and Background Properties	53
Box Properties	44
Classification Properties	48

Units

Unit data enables properties such as color and size to work. There are many unit options from which to choose. Be creative when developing a Web site. Do you want your site to blend in? Or do you want your site to "stand up on the teacher's desk and demand the attention of the entire class." You decide. Oh, by the way, don't go overboard!

To learn more about...	Go to page...
Length Units	94
Percentage Units	137
Color Units	54

Commands

This quick table directs you to the most commonly used elements in CSS1. The elements are organized by category, which helps you to quickly locate the element you want and helps you save the time that you would normally spend looking through the index.

Commands

To find the commands for...	Go to page...
Fonts	69-79
Color and Background	53
Box Properties	44
Lists	100
Links and Graphics	10, 99

Fonts

This is what it's all about: The ability to manipulate fonts. Check out the following sections on font manipulation and let your imagination be your guide. This table will direct you to the appropriate pages for specifics on fonts.

Font Element...	Go to page...
font	69
font-family	70
font-size	74
font-style	77
font-weight	79
line-height	98

Color and Background

Most Web pages contain a background color or image. Many use inline color manipulation to highlight portions of the document.

Style sheets also allow for manipulation of background and text color. Style sheets provide you with many more options, yet require less typing.

Color Element...	Go to page...
background	29
color	52
Color Values	54, 185

Box Properties

The Box properties set the layout of a page—margins, borders, padding, and so on. Use this table to optimize your page appearance through the manipulation of box properties.

Properties...	Go to page...
border	33
clear	49
float	68
height	82
margin	107
padding	127
width	173

Lists

Add new elements to the appearance of your lists `<LI>` display (disc, upper & lower roman, and so on).

Lists...	Go to page...
circle	47
decimal	60
disc	61
Lists	100
list-style	102

Links and Graphics

CSS1 enhances the developer's control over the appearance of a Web site. Use this table to quickly find elements that are associated with links and graphics in CSS1.

Elements	Go to page...
A	21
active	26
BODY	33
border	33
IMG	85
list-style	102

User-Defined Style Sheets

Understanding the potential control users may have over the presentation of your work allows you to create more effective style sheets. Read this section to understand the limits placed on a user's or author's style sheets.

UNDERSTANDING THE HTML CSS QUICK REFERENCE SECTION

In the "HTML CSS Quick Reference Section," you will find a complete and exhaustive command reference for all of the major style sheet elements and their related HTML usage.

The HTML style sheet elements in this section are in alphanumeric sort, as you would expect to find in an encyclopedia. A figure is sometimes provided to help illustrate the effect caused by the use of that element.

Every effort has been made to build the most comprehensive and up-to-date reference source for the HTML style sheet language, CSS. You should note, however, that this language is still in its infancy and expectations are that several additions will be made to the language. The growth of the HTML style sheet language should be very similar to the manner in which HTML has grown from its early, text-only language to its current status. There will likely be extensions to CSS1 to support non-visual media (such as speech and Braille output), more precise font specifications, and an extension to the color names.

New elements will be added to subsequent editions of this book as they are recognized, adopted, and implemented in commercial browsers, or included in subsequent HTML Cascading Style Sheet standards.

This reference guide attempts to document every HTML style sheet element you may run across. However, individual attributes will not always be represented by specific entries. A few element/attribute combinations are important enough to merit a specific entry and, therefore, have been granted one.

Don't forget to check the Macmillan Computer Publishing Web site at **http://www.mcp.com/que/books** for updates on subsequent releases of this book and other HTML reference books.

HTML Style Sheet Categories

Most of the HTML style sheet elements in this book are grouped into families or functional categories, which should make the learning process much easier for you. You should be able to clearly identify the relationship each element has with the style sheet. To develop a successful style sheet, it is necessary to understand the proper placement of the elements in your style sheet.

The specific categories that are defined in the "HTML CSS Quick Reference Section" are the same categories that appeared in the "Quick Tables" section at the beginning of this book. Some additional categories have been added where the area or topic is important enough to warrant an individual category.

As the CSS specifications mature, individual categories are expected to proliferate and become areas of specialty for many HTML authors. The following sections describe those categories.

Basic Concepts

This category includes everything needed to start using CSS. You must fully understand the CSS document before you can properly author it. These basic concepts will be useful for writing your first style sheet. A few of the basic concepts presented include the BODY element, cascading order, and containment in HTML.

Pseudo

Pseudo-classes and pseudo-elements pick up where HTML left off by providing for addressing from the HTML document to the style sheet source. Pseudo-elements address sub-parts of elements and pseudo-classes enable style sheets to differentiate between element types.

Box Properties

The Box Properties category includes vertical and horizontal formatting, list properties, and so on. This category is used for defining the browser canvas (appearance).

Font

Under the Font category, you will find the various elements used for setting font properties. `font-size`, `font-weight`, and `font-family` are some examples of font properties.

Color and Background

The Color and Background category includes such things as colored text, images on the background of the Web page, and a scrolling background. There are many ways to manipulate the appearance of your Web site. This category includes all of the elements of color and background in CSS.

Text

This category consists of the elements required to manipulate the presentation of text dynamically, which includes such elements as `text-indent`, `text-transform`, and `line-height`.

Units

Number and color units are described in this section. These units are used to instruct the browser exactly how to display the affected properties. `font-size`, `margin`, and `color` are some examples of elements that require a unit value.

Lists

Lists include data that is sorted and organized according to the author's specifications, with list items clearly identified by a marker (unless the author sets the `list-style` property at none). All related elements for lists are included in this category. CSS has added `list-style`.

Links and Graphics

Links take the reader to another point in the page or to another document. Links can be combined with properties from other categories, such as `text-decoration`. Graphics are images that are included in the document and displayed by the browser.

The HTML Style Sheet Reference Section

The "HTML Style Sheet Reference Section" describes HTML style sheet attributes. Some elements occupy more than a single page, which is required to document them properly. The information you will find for every element included in the "HTML Style Sheet Reference Section" is categorized under the following six headings.

Command Header

This section displays the name of the HTML Style Sheet element that is described on that page or pages.

Syntax

Example syntax for the element is provided under this heading to show how the element is used. These examples are *not* taken from actual style sheets nor are they intended for such use. Real examples are provided under the "Example Syntax" heading.

Definition

Under this heading, you will find a definition that describes the original, intended use for the element. Any general discussion of the element appears in this section. A table also may be included in the definition section if there are values relevant to the topic.

Example Syntax

This section provides an example of how the element is used in an actual line of an HTML document. Also, if a figure is displayed on the same page, every effort has been made to display the result of the "Example Syntax" in that figure.

Related Attributes Table

All elements with optional related attributes will have a table which refers the reader to the related attributes.

Related Topics Table

Most of the elements will have a Related Topics Table, which informs the reader of related CSS1/HTML topics that can be used outside or inside the discussed element.

HTML Style Sheet Compliance

Microsoft's Internet Explorer is the first CSS1 compatible commercial browser. Although not all Cascading Style Sheet elements are supported by MSIE 3.01 for Windows 95, Microsoft has indicated that it will fully support the W3C specifications in the near future. In the Reference Section of this book, any CSS element that is supported by MSIE 3.01 will have the Microsoft Internet Explorer icon (shown above) located to the right of the element name.

This Quick Reference includes those aspects of CSS that constitute the basic requirements of a CSS browser, according to the CSS developers. It is important to remember that CSS is still in its infancy and, therefore, is susceptible to change.

In the last year, there have been many changes to HTML. Expectations are that, over the next year, many more changes will occur to both HTML and CSS. CSS intends to include better paper printing support, speech and Braille output, more color names, greater font specification, and expects more attributes to be added by the browser vendors.

STYLE SHEETS
REFERENCE SECTION

/*

Syntax

/ * ... * /

Definition

The / * * / element allows the author of an HTML style sheet to place comments in the code, which can only be seen while editing the document.

Category

Basic Concepts

Example Syntax

```
/* The comment section can be written as one line.
 * Or it can be composed of many lines.  It cannot
be embedded.
*/
```

Related Topics...	Go to page...
comment	55
<!--	20

<!--

Syntax

```
<!--...-->
```

Definition

In HTML, the <!-- element is used to mark comments. This element is also used to hide the <style> element from non-CSS compliant browsers. Normally, a browser that does not support CSS will ignore the <style> elements and process the data between the unrecognized elements as text. This has an extremely undesirable effect on the appearance of the Web page.

Category

Basic Concepts

Example Syntax

```
<!--
<STYLE  TYPE="text/css">
BODY  { background:white;
color: black }
-->
```

Related Topics...	Go to page...
/*	19
BODY	33
comment	7, 55
P	126
SPAN	150
STYLE	152

Syntax

```
A:
```

Definition

The A element, commonly referred to as the anchor element, shows the user which portion of the site is hyperlinked. The user's browser remembers which links have been visited and displays them differently (depending on the style written) the next time the user returns to that page.

Category

Links and Graphics

Example Syntax

```
A:link    { text-decoration:none;
            color:blue;
            font-size: 10pt;
            font-weight: bold
      }       /*  Unvisited link information is
                  set as stated  */

A:visited    { color:#00009c; text-decoration:line-
              through; font-size: 8pt;
              font-weight: bold
      }       /*  Visited link will have a strike
                  through  */
-- >
</STYLE>
</HEAD>
<BODY>
<p>
<center>
<h6>LINKS</h6>
  <a href="http://www.hwg.org">HTML Writers
  Guild</A> {HWG} <br>
```

```
<a href="http://www.w3.org">W3C</A> <br>
<a href="http://www.cwebdev.com">Crystal Web
Designs</A> <br>
<a href="http://www.netroute.net">Canadian
ISP</A><br>
<a href="www.que.mcp.com">www.que.mcp.com</a> <br>
<a href="www.ladydars.com">www.ladydars.com</a>

</center>
</p>
```

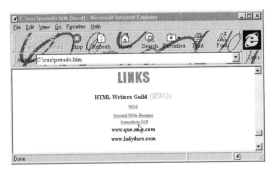

Fig. 1 This is the result of the example syntax.

Related Attributes...	Go to page...
active	26
LINK	99
VISITED	172

Related Topics...	Go to page...
Anchor Pseudo-classes	27
BODY	33
Color	52
Font	15, 69

Related Topics...	Go to page...
IMG	85
TEXT	15
text-decoration	157

Absolute Length Units

Syntax

[in] | [cm] | [mm] | [pt] | [pc] | [px]

Definition

The preceding ALUs (Absolute Length Units) are used to specify length values. The ALUs are only appropriate when the physical output is known, as with a monitor or printer.

Category

Font

Example Syntax

```
P {font-size: 12mm}
➡/* sets the font to the indicated size
according to value */
```

Related Attributes...	Go to page...
cm	50
mm	119
pc	135
pt	140
px	142

Absolute Length Units

Related Topics...	Go to page...
width	173
word-spacing	174

Absolute Size

Syntax

... {font-size:[xx-small] | [x-small]
[small] | [medium] | [large] | [x-large] | [xx-large] }

Definition

An absolute size keyword tells the browser to look up and compute the font size. The list is already in the browser and is formatted accordingly. In the example below, the font size is set to xx-large. Unless otherwise stated, all child elements will inherit that element.

The scaling factor between sizes is about 1.5. If medium were 10pt, large would be 15pt.

Category

font

Example Syntax

P {font-size: xx-large }

Keywords

large

medium

small

x-large

continues

Absolute Size

continued

Keywords
x-small
xx-large
xx-small

Related Topics...	Go to page...
BLOCKQUOTE	32
em	64
font-size	74
H1-H6	81
P	126

active

Syntax

a:active

Definition

active is used to define the appearance of a link that is active (visible while waiting for the link to resolve).

In CSS this can be manipulated with color, font, and text decoration elements to ensure continuity in the overall appearance of the page.

Category

links and graphics

Example Syntax

```
A: active {color: red}
```

Related Attributes...	Go to page...
A	21
Anchor Pseudo-classes	27
LINK	99
VISITED	172

Related Topics...	Go to page...
BODY	33
color	52
IMG	85

Anchor Pseudo-classes

Syntax

```
A: [link (element)]|[visited]|[active]
```

Definition (element)

Anchor pseudo-classes are used to create CSS hyperlink attributes such as color and font.

In the next example, the link pseudo-class is set with size, color, and font-family.

Category

Links and Graphics

Example Syntax

```
A: link { color: green;
size: 15px;
font-family: Impact}
```

Related Attributes...	Go to page...
A	21
active	26
LINK	99
VISITED	172

auto

Syntax

... { [margin-...]|[padding-...][|width]|[height] : auto}

Definition

When the value is set to `auto` for one of the previously mentioned properties, the browser automatically formats the property based on the other information it has for that element.

You must provide at least one reference point for the browser. See the example syntax that follows.

Category

Box properties

Example Syntax

```
img.shorty { width: 60px;
height: auto }
```

background

Syntax

... {background: ...}

Definition

The background of a Web site is normally a solid color or an image. Why would it be anything else in CSS? Because CSS is *not* HTML.

With CSS, you can position an image in a particular location over the top of a solid color, make the image remain in that one position (like a letter head), or follow the contents of the page.

You can then tell the browser to repeat the image horizontally (repeat-x) or vertically (repeat-y), to cover the canvas (repeat), or to specify no-repeat.

If you do specify an image as your background, in addition to setting a background color and deciding whether you want the image to repeat, you also have to specify whether the image should scroll (scroll), or if it should remain stationary (fixed).

Now you can position your background image almost anywhere you want. Use the following table as your key to background positioning.

background

Key to positioning...	Percentages...	Keywords...
Top	0%	top
Center	50%	center
Bottom	100%	bottom
Left	0%	left
Right	100%	right
Upper left	0% 0%	top left
Center top	0% 50%	top center
Center left	50% 0%	center left
Center right	50% 100%	center right
Center bottom	100% 50%	bottom center
Bottom left	100% 0%	bottom left
Bottom right	100% 100%	bottom right

Category

Color and Backgrounds

Example Syntax

```
BODY { background: http://www.cwebdev.com/mypic.jpg
right top }
```

Related Attributes...	Go to page...
color	52
Position	139
repeat	144
scroll	147

baseline

Syntax

...{vertical-align: baseline}

Definition

The baseline value of vertical-align is used to align the baseline of the element with the parent.

Applies to in-line and replaced elements only.

Category

font

Example Syntax

```
kewl {vertical-align: baseline }
<B CLASS=kewl>Your BOLD Text </B>is vertically
aligned with the baseline of the parent element.
```

Related Attributes...	Go to page...
vertical-align	170

BLOCKQUOTE

Syntax

BLOCKQUOTE {...}

Definition

BLOCKQUOTE is a block level element (line break before and after element) that is indented on the left and right.

Category

Box Properties

Example Syntax

BLOCKQUOTE {font-size: 15pt}

Related Attributes...	Go to page...
border	33
border-bottom	35
border-left	36
border-right	38
border-top	41
border-width	42
margin	107
margin-bottom	109
margin-left	110
margin-right	112
margin-top	114
padding	127
padding-bottom	129
padding-left	130

Related Attributes...	Go to page...
padding-right	132
padding-top	134

BODY

Syntax

BODY {...}

Definition

BODY is the parent of all elements in the style sheet. It is also the element in which you specify the background and foreground properties for the entire document or group of documents, whichever the case may be.

Category

Basic Concepts

Example Syntax

BODY {background: green}

border

Syntax

... { border: ...}

Definition

border draws a border on all four sides of the element to which it is attached.

border

Category

Box Properties

Example Syntax

```
H1 {border: groove thin green}
```

Related Attributes...	Go to page...
border-style	39
border-width	42
color	52

Related Topics...	Go to page...
border-bottom	35
border-left	36
border-right	38
border-top	41
IMG	85
LINK	99
List	15, 100
margin	107
margin-bottom	109
margin-left	110
margin-right	112
margin-top	114
P	126
padding	127
padding-bottom	129
padding-left	130

Related Topics...	Go to page...
padding-right	132
padding-top	134

border-bottom

Syntax

... {border-bottom: ... }

Definition

border-bottom draws the border for the bottom of the element to which it is attached.

Category

Box Properties

Example Syntax

H1 {border-bottom: double red}

Related Attributes...	Go to page...
border-style	39
border-width	42
color	52

Related Topics...	Go to page...
border	33
border-left	36

continues

border-bottom

continued

Related Topics...	Go to page...
border-right	38
border-top	41
IMG	85
LINK	99
List	15, 100
margin	107
margin-bottom	109
margin-left	110
margin-right	112
margin-top	114
padding	127
padding-bottom	129
padding-left	130
padding-right	132
padding-top	134

border-left

Syntax

... {border-left: ... }

Definition

border-left draws the left border for the element to which
it is attached.

Category

Box Properties

Example Syntax

`P {border-left: solid blue}`

Related Attributes...	Go to page...
border-style	39
border-width	42
color	52

Related Topics...	Go to page...
border	33
border-bottom	35
border-right	38
border-top	41
border-width	42
IMG	85
LINK	99
List	15, 100
margin	107
margin-bottom	109
margin-left	110
margin-right	112
margin-top	114
padding	127
padding-bottom	129
padding-left	130
padding-right	132
padding-top	134

border-right

Syntax

... {border-right: ... }

Definition

border-right draws the right border for the element to which it is attached.

Category

Box Properties

Example Syntax

H1 {border-right: thin }

Related Attributes...	Go to page...
border-style	39
border-width	42
color	52

Related Topics...	Go to page...
border	33
border-bottom	35
border-left	36
border-top	41
border-width	42
IMG	85
LINK	99
List	15, 100

border-style

Syntax

```
... {border:
[none] | [dotted] | [dashed] | [solid] [double] [groove] | [ridge] | [inset] | [outset] }
```

Definition

The `border-style` property defines the style in which the border is drawn. As demonstrated in the next table, there are many styles from which to choose. Experiment with these styles to familiarize yourself with their characteristics.

Category

Box Properties

Example Syntax

```
H1 {border: ridge red}
```

border-style

border-top

Syntax

... {border-top: ... }

Definition

The border-top property draws the top border of the element to which it is attached.

Category

Box Properties

Example Syntax

H1 {border-top: solid}

Related Attributes...	Go to page...
border-style	39
border-width	42
color	52

Related Topics...	Go to page...
border	33
border-bottom	35
border-left	36
border-right	38
border-width	42
IMG	85
LINK	99
List	15, 100
margin	107
margin-bottom	109
margin-left	110
margin-right	112
margin-top	114
padding	127
padding-bottom	129
padding-left	130
padding-right	132
padding-top	134

border-width

Syntax

... {border: [thin]|[medium]|[thick]}

Definition

The border-width property defines the width of the border. It does not necessarily define the width of all sides.

If, for example, you set the `border-width` dimensions of the top, the remaining sides will take their cue from those dimensions and format accordingly.

The default attribute for `border-width` is `medium`.

Category

Box Properties

Example Syntax

```
P {border: double thick}
```

Related Attributes...	Go to page...
border-style	39
color	52
length	94
medium	116
thick	162
thin	164

Related Topics...	Go to page...
border	33
border-bottom	35
border-left	36
border-right	38
border-top	41
IMG	85
LINK	99
List	15, 100

continues

border-width

continued

Related Topics...	Go to page...
margin	107
margin-bottom	109
margin-left	110
margin-right	112
margin-top	114
padding	127
padding-bottom	129
padding-left	130
padding-right	132
padding-top	134

Box Properties

Syntax

... { [margin] | [padding] | [border] | [width] |
➡ [height] | [float] | [clear]

Definition

Box Properties are the CSS properties that make up the different aspects of an element. A list would have a box around it. The box may or may not be shown. Each box consists of the height and width of the element, as well as the margin, padding, and the border.

Category

Box Properties

Example Syntax

Related Attributes...	Go to page...
border	33
border-bottom	35
border-left	36
border-right	38
border-style	39
border-top	41
border-width	42
clear	49
float	68
height	82
margin	107
margin-bottom	109
margin-left	110
margin-right	112
margin-top	114
padding	127
padding-bottom	129
padding-left	130
padding-right	132
padding-top	134
width	173

capitalize

Syntax

... { text-transform: capitalize }

Definition

Using text-transform, the capitalize attribute transforms the appearance of the first letter of each word in the element to a capital letter.

Category

text

Example Syntax

H1 {text-transform: capitalize}

Related Attributes...	Go to page...
lowercase	104
none	122
uppercase	169

Cascading Order

Syntax

Not applicable

Definition

The cascading order is the order of operations for CSS.

The browser first reads and interprets all declarations related to the element, and then it sorts the declarations by weight, normal, or

`!important`. The browser next determines the origin of the style sheet as to whether it originates from the author or reader, and then sorts by selector. Finally, the selectors are sorted by the order specified. If there is more than one attribute specified, and all are legal attributes of the same weight, the last legal attribute specified will be used.

Category

Basic Concepts

Example Syntax

Not applicable

circle

Syntax

`… {list-style: circle}`

Definition

A circle is one of the possible shapes that is used to mark the list item in the `<UL>` HTML element.

Category

Lists

Example Syntax

`UL LI { list-style: circle }`

Related Attributes...	Go to page...
decimal	60
disc	61
lower-alpha	105
lower-roman	106

continues

circle

continued

Related Attributes...	Go to page...
none	122
square	151
upper-alpha	167
upper-roman	168

Class as Selector

Syntax

```
... .classname   {...: ...}
```

Definition

Using the CLASS element, you can make any HTML element perform any function you wish. The element is so powerful that you can make a element emulate the function of another element. You can effectively write an entire HTML document with very little actual HTML. Remember, having the power doesn't necessarily mean you should use it. Keep in mind the present environment of the Web when developing a site.

Category

Basic Concepts

Example Syntax

```
.oct   {font:50px fantasy;
           margin-bottom:-20px; }
.test   {font-size:160%;
           margin-bottom:-6px;
           margin-top:-6px;
        text-indent:15px}
.scaps   {font-size:60%;  margin-bottom:6px}
-- >
```

```
</STYLE>
</HEAD>
<BODY>
<center>
<B class="oct">The October Comet</B><!-- Copyright
1996 James R. Falla -->
</center>
<p>
<b class="test">A</B><b class="scaps">LL EYES
LOOKED TO THE SKY</b> as an enormous comet hurtled
to the earth leaving an eerie green trail in
its wake. It appeared to those watching that the
comet slammed down just beyond the town to the
east. Within minutes a parade of cars, trucks and
bicycles were heading down Deer Park Rd. towards
the imagined crash site.  </p>
```

Fig. 2 This is the result of the example syntax.

clear

Syntax

... {clear: ... }

Definition

The clear property instructs the browser not to place floating elements on left, right, both, or the default value of none, which is the same as not placing the clear property in the code.

clear

If you want to ensure that the browser doesn't place a floating image to the left of a paragraph, for example, you would say

```
P.CLEAR {clear : left }  /* The class name is
CLEAR */
```

Category

Box Properties

Example Syntax

```
H1 {clear: both }
➥/*  no floating elements are allowed on either
side of H1  */
```

Related Attributes...	Go to page...
none	122

Related Topics...	Go to page...
BLOCKQUOTE	32
BODY	33
CLASS	48
float	68
H1–H6	81
List	15, 100
P	126

cm

Syntax

```
… {…: …cm}
```

Definition

cm (centimeters) is used for formatting length values like width, text-width, etc.

Category

Units

Example Syntax

P {line-height: 2cm }

Related Attributes...	Go to page...
auto	28
em	64
ex	66
mm	119
pc	135
pt	140
px	142

Related Topics...	Go to page...
border	33
border-bottom	35
border-left	36
border-right	38
border-top	41
border-width	42
font-size	74

continues

continued

Related Topics...	Go to page...
height	82
letter-spacing	96
line-height	98
margin	107
margin-bottom	109
margin-left	110
margin-right	112
margin-top	114
padding	127
padding-bottom	129
padding-left	130
padding-right	132
padding-top	134
width	173
word-spacing	174

color

Syntax

    ... {color: ... }

Definition

color defines the color of text, borders, background, and foreground. See the Color Table in Appendix B for more detailed color property information.

Category

Color & Background

Example Syntax

H1 { color: green }

Related Topics...	Go to page...
border	33
Color Values	54
font	69
H1–H6	81
P	126
Text	15

Color and Background Properties

Syntax

Not applicable

Definition

The background and colors are defined by the rules set out in this category. To learn more about this category, refer to the next table.

Category

Colors and Backgrounds

Example Syntax

Not applicable

Color and Background Properties

Related Attributes...	Go to page...
A	21
background	29
border-bottom	35
border-left	36
border-right	38
border-top	41
border-width	42
color	52
font	69
margin	107
margin-bottom	109
margin-left	110
margin-right	112
margin-top	114
padding	127
padding-bottom	129
padding-left	130
padding-right	132
padding-top	134

Color Values

Syntax

```
#ff2400 | gold
➥/* then the RGB value or the color name can be
used. */
```

Definition

Colors can be referred to by either the color name or the RGB value. For examples of the different ways color can be specified, refer to the color tables in Appendix B.

Category

Color and Background

Example Syntax

```
BODY { background: #ffffff;

color: black }

/* the background would be white and the text color
black */
```

Related Attributes...	Go to page...
color	52
Color and Background	8, 53

Comments

Syntax

```
/*    */
```

Definition

Placing comments in the tag is a good idea for anyone, especially those new to CSS. Comments make it much easier to find and edit less obvious code items.

Category

Basic Concepts

Comments

Example Syntax

```
/* comments go here. Comments cannot be put in-line
with text.  */
```

Containment in HTML

Syntax

```
Not applicable
```

Definition

You can place the style sheet data directly in the head of the document if it is for a single Web page. If you are working with a site larger than one HTML page, use the @import option or the LINK element.

Using the @import attribute, you can affect the presentation of many HTML pages from a single style sheet.

Using LINK is very similar to using @import and is probably better than using @import. LINK references alternative style sheets from which the reader can select. Imported style sheets simply merge, following the cascading order, with any other style sheets.

The final option is to place style attributes directly in the <BODY> of the document. You have to use the HTML <SPAN> element to do this. The benefit of using this option is that you can change one particular element without having to add a new pseudo-class, or you can change the presentation of all other instances of that element.

Category

Basic concepts

Example Syntax

```
<HTML>
<HEAD>
<LINK REL=STYLESHEET  TYPE="text/css"
  HREF="http://www.cwebdev.com/example.css"
TITLE="example">
<STYLE TYPE="text/css">
```

```
<!--
    @import url(http://www.cwebdev.com/example.css)
    BODY {background:white;
    color:black}
    H1 {color="#ca0000"}
</STYLE>
</HEAD>
<BODY>
    <H1>Heading is off blue</H1>
    <SPAN STYLE="color:blue">
    <P>The paragraph, or any other elements will
➥be blue.
    <P>This paragraph is also blue.
    </SPAN>
    <H1 SYYLE="border:dashed thick green">
You can also do one element at a time.
</BODY>
</HTML>
```

Contextual Selectors

Syntax

[ancestor] [element]   {... : ... }

Definition

Due to the inherent nature of CSS, you are not required to set all style properties. By using contextual selectors, you can determine the default style settings; then, using the selector element, you can list the exceptions to the defined styles.

Contextual selectors work on the inherited element principle, which means that selectors will only work *if* there is an ancestor element; in other words, UL UL LI {font-size: x-small}.

The LI element in the above example is defined as having a font size set at extra small. The sub-list UL UL LI will inherit all the defined features of UL LI except font-size information, which is defined by the contextual selector.

Contextual Selectors

Here's how it works: Only the last selector (LI in the previous example) is addressed. Only elements that match the **search criteria** (UL UL in the example) are effected. UL LI would not be effected by this contextual selector. The sub-list UL UL criteria must be met, or else this contextual selector will have no effect on the document.

You can use elements, classes, and IDs with contextual selectors. You also can group together several contextual selectors that have the same output. They must be separated by a coma, i.e., H1 B, H2 B {...}

Category

Basic Concepts

Example Syntax

```
UL {background:gold;  list-style:none;
        font:16px fantasy;
        color:#424263
        }
UL LI { border:dashed thick green;
        margin:3px;
        padding:1px;
        font:15px Western
        }
UL LI LI  {    font: 12px         } /* the second
level LI will be 12px */
OL  {background:yellow; list-style:roman;
        font: 18px Western;
        color:#424263
        }
OL LI LI { font-size:12px}
OL LI LI LI {font:10px courier new}
-- >
</STYLE>
</HEAD>
<BODY>
<ol><li>List item
<ul><li>new font with drop levels
<ol><li>you can also use a different font-family
</li></ol></li>
<li>The more you put into it
<ol><li>The more you get out of it.
```

```
</li></ol></li></ul></li>
<br>See for yourself<br>
<li>second
<ul><li>CSS EXTENXIBILITY
</li>
<ol><li>Etc ...  (just try it!)</li></ol></ul></li>
<hr>
```

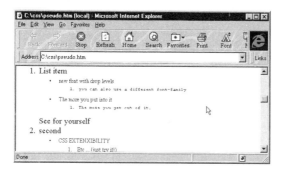

Fig. 3   This is the result of the example syntax.

dashed

Syntax

... {border: dashed }

Definition

dashed draws a dashed border around the selected element. By using other elements, you can change the size and color of the border.

Category

Box Properties

Example Syntax

H1 {border: dashed thick }

dashed

Related Attributes...	Go to page...
border	33
border-bottom	35
border-left	36
border-right	38
border-style	39
border-top	41
border-width	42
dotted	62
double	63
groove	80
inset	92
none	122
outset	124
ridge	146
solid	148

decimal

Syntax

... {list-style: decimal }

Definition

list-style: decimal will return a numerical (1 2 3 4...) value to
<OL> list items.

Category

Lists

Example Syntax

```
OL {list-style: decimal}
```

Related Attributes...	Go to page...
circle	47
disc	61
lower-alpha	105
lower-roman	106
none	122
square	151
upper-alpha	167
upper-roman	168

disc

Syntax

```
... {list-style: disc}
```

Definition

list-style disc will produce a disc on <UL> list items.

Category

Lists

Example Syntax

```
UL {list-style: disc}
```

disc

Related Attributes...	Go to page...
circle	47
decimal	60
lower-alpha	105
lower-roman	106
none	122
square	151
upper-alpha	167
upper-roman	168

dotted

Syntax

... { border: dotted }

Definition

dotted draws a dotted border around the selected element.

Category

Box Properties

Example Syntax

TABLE {border: dotted }

Related Attributes...	Go to page...
border	33
border-bottom	35
border-left	36

double

Syntax

... {border: double}

Definition

double inserts two single lines, drawn at the edges of the border-width.

Category

Box Properties

Example Syntax

... {border: double }

double

em

Syntax

... {...: ...em }

Definition

em is a relative unit that is drawn relative to the parent element font. Put another way, an em is the height of the element's font.

Category

Units

Example Syntax

... {margin:.5em }

Relative Attributes...	Go to page...
auto	28
cm	50
ex	66
mm	119
pc	135
pt	140
px	142

Related Topics...	Go to page...
border	33
font-size	74
height	82
letter-spacing	96
line-height	98
margin	107
padding	127
width	173
word-spacing	174

ex

Syntax

... {...:...ex }

Definition

ex means x-height; the height of the letter *x*. This is a relative size element.

Category

Units

Example Syntax

H1 {margin:1.5ex}

Related Attributes...	Go to page...
auto	28
cm	50
em	64
mm	119
pc	135
pt	140
px	142

Related Topics...	Go to page...
border	33
font-size	74
height	82

first-letter

Syntax

```
P:first-letter { ...:... }
```

Definition

A common feature of print publishing is to see the first letter of an article, chapter, book, or whatever it may be, much larger than the rest of the text. This can be quite effective with print media—why not add it to the Web?

The first letter element is as old as the written word. Thousands of years ago, scholars worked for hours on the first letter of their writings. With the potential of the text-decoration properties, who knows.... It is only fitting that this ancient tool of the trade should make the transition to electronic publishing.

Category

Pseudo-elements

Example Syntax

```
P:first-letter { ...:... }
</HEAD>
<BODY>
```

```
<P>
<P:first-letter> F </P:first-line>irst letter.
bla bla bla
</P>
```

first-line

Syntax

```
P:first-line { ...:... }
```

Definition

This is one of the pseudo-elements. First-line will set the first line of text apart from the rest of the paragraph. It can be used to make the first line of text all uppercase.

Category

Pseudo-elements

Example Syntax

```
P:first-line { ...:... }
</HEAD>
<BODY>
<P>
<P:first-line> bla bla bla </P:first-line>
bla bla bla
</P>
```

float

Syntax

```
... {float: [left]|[right]|[none]}
```

Definition

The `float` element makes the image float to the left or right of the text or, using the value of none, the image will be displayed where it appears in the text.

Note: Expect to soon see some sort of `wrap` value added to this element.

Category

Box Properties

Example Syntax

`IMG.set {float:left}`

Related Attributes...	Go to page...
none	122

font

Syntax

`... {font: ... }`

Definition

`font` is the catch-all for font properties. The `font` element allows you to set style data for the `font-size`, `line-height`, and `font-family`.

If you leave out any of the elements, the initial value will be assumed by the browser.

font

Category

Font

Example Syntax

... {font: ... }

Related Attributes...	Go to page...
font-family	70
Font-Matching	72
font-size	74
font-style	77
font-variant	78
font-weight	79

font-family

Syntax

... {font-family: ... }

Definition

The font-family element offers you the option to specify alternative family names, separated by a comma.

Not all browsers will offer all fonts. It is for this reason that style sheet designers should specify alternatives. The last alternative should be a generic-family name.

Category

Font

Example Syntax

```
H1 {font:30px Courier new}
H2 {font:30px Courier}
H3  {font:30px fantasy }
H4  {font:30px Western}
H5  {font:30px Helvetica}
H6  {font:30px Impact}


TABLE    {background:yellow;
          color:blue;
        }    /* the background is yellow and the
text is blue  */
-- >
</STYLE>
</HEAD>
<BODY>
<center>
<p>The following are examples of various fonts.
The font-size for each is 30px </p>
</center>
<table  border=1  width=100%>
<tr><td><center>
<H1>Courier new</H1>
</center></td>
<td><center>
<h2>Courier</h2>
</center></td></tr>
<tr><td><center>
<h3>Fantasy</h3>
</center></td>
<td><center>
<h4>Western</h4>
</center></td></tr>
<tr><td><center>
```

```
<h5>Helvetica</h5>
</center></td>
<td><center>
<h6>Impact</h6>
</center></td></tr>
</table><br><br>
<hr solid>
```

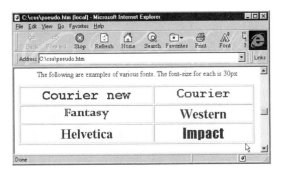

Fig. 4 Here are some example fonts.

Font Matching

Syntax

Not applicable

Definition

The browser looks in its font database for a font with the name specified. If there is no match, it moves on to the first alternative and tries again, and so on.

Once the browser decides on the proper family, it starts to work on font-style, font-variant, font-weight, and font-size, in that order.

It's a good idea to take font matching into consideration when designing a style sheet.

Category

Font

Example Syntax

Not applicable

Font Properties

Syntax

Not applicable

Font Properties

Definition

Font properties are all of the elements and values in the font category. Use care when defining font settings. Refer to the appropriate font topics to ensure the settings are correct.

Category

Font

Example Syntax

Not applicable

Related Topics...	Go to page...
font-family	70
Font-Matching	72
font-size	74
font-style	77
font-variant	78
font-weight	79

font-size

Syntax

```
... { font-size: ... }
```

Definition

This property defines the size of the font. You can have an `absolute-size` or a `relative-size`, and you can specify the `length` and `percentage` values relative to parent element font sizes.

Category

Font

Example Syntax

```
.large{font-size:130%}
.supp{font-size:60%}
-->
</STYLE>
</HEAD>
<BODY>
<p>

It has been said that<b class="supp"> there are no
advantages</b> to having a web site on the
Internet.  The advantage is there. It's up to the
web developer to <b class="large">find and ex-
ploit</b> the opportunities.
</p>

<p>
<b class="large">The thing to remember</b> when
designing your site is content is at least as
important as presentation style.  Use all the bells
and whistles you want, just make sure the site is
worth all the <b class="supp">HYPE</b>.
```

font-size

Fig. 5 This is the result of the example syntax.

Related Attributes...	Go to page...
Absolute-Size	25
length	94
percentage	137

Related Topics...	Go to page...
font-family	70
Font-Matching	72
font-style	77
font-variant	78
font-weight	79
Font Properties	73

font-style

Syntax

... `{font-style: [normal]|[italic]|[oblique] }`

Definition

`font-style` allows the designer to choose a style of `normal,` `italic,` or `oblique.` The value names are searched for in the browser database, based on the `font-family` specified. A `font-style` of `normal` displays the text in the roman (upright) font style. The `italic` and `oblique` fonts are explained in more detail later in the chapter.

Category

Font

Example Syntax

`EM   { font-style: italic }`

Related Attributes...	Go to page...
italic	93
normal	123
oblique	123

Related Topics...	Go to page...
H1-H6	81
P	126

font-variant

Syntax

```
...   {font-variant:   [normal]|[small-caps]   }
```

Definition

The font-variant property allows the designer to select a variant
of normal or small-caps. In the event the browser can't find a font
in small capitals, it will display all uppercase as a replacement for
small-caps.

Category

Font

Example Syntax

```
P   { font-variant: small-caps }
```

Related Attributes...	Go to page...
normal	123

Related Topics...	Go to page...
P	126
H1-H6	81
normal	123

font-weight

Syntax

... { font-weight:[normal]|[bold]|[bolder]|[lighter]
|[100]|[200]|[300]|[400]|[500]|[600]|[700]|[800]|[900] }

Definition

The weight of a font is actually the darkness of its shading. In other words, if you select a normal font, the text will appear in a standard shade. If you select bold, the text's font will be a much darker shade. Font 400 is the same as normal font and font 700 is the same as bold.

There are a total of nine different font shades, or font-weight options, from which to choose.

The exception to this general rule is bolder and lighter. These font-weight values are relative weight options. These weight options are relative to the weight inherited from the parent elements.

Category

Font

Example Syntax

... {font-weight: 500 }

Related Attributes...	Go to page...
Lists	100
normal	123

Related Topics...	Go to page...
H1-H6	81
P	126

groove

Syntax

... {border: groove}

Definition

A 3-D groove style border is drawn around the element using the color value selected.

Category

Box Properties

Example Syntax

H1 {border: groove}

Related Attributes...	Go to page...
border	33
clear	49
float	68
height	82

margin	107
padding	127
width	173

Grouping

Syntax

... , ... , ...   { ...:... ,   ...:...   }

Definition

This is what style sheets are all about—the ability to group lots of style sheet information into only a few separate entries. *Remember: style declarations must be separated by a comma.*

Category

Basic Concepts

Example Syntax

H1, H2, H3 { font-style: normal }

Headings (H1-H6)

Syntax

[H1] | [H2] | [H3] | [H4] | [H5] | [H6] {   ...:...   }

Definition

Headings are block level elements that are formatted in a slightly different manner from the rest of the text. Style sheets allow the designer to determine exactly what each heading will look like.

Category

Basic Concepts

Example Syntax

```
H1   {font-style: normal}
```

height

Syntax

```
...  { height:... }
```

Definition

`height` applies to block-level and replaced elements such as images. This property is specifically intended for setting height values but can also be applied to text.

Category

Box Properties

Example Syntax

```
P   { height: 20pt }
```

Related Attributes...	Go to page...
auto	28
length	94

Related Topics...	Go to page...
border	33
border-bottom	35
border-left	36

Horizontal Formatting

Syntax

```
...   {   padding-right:  ...  }
```

Definition

The horizontal dimensions of the box are `margin-left, border-left, padding-left, width, padding-right, border-right,` and `margin-right`.

The sum of these properties must equal the width of the parent element. If they do not, one property must be set to auto.

If you are using the float property, which also contains its own values (left, right, and none), the margin must be set to

```
float:left;    margin-right:auto
float:right    margin-left:auto
```

Category

Box Properties

Example Syntax

```
H1  { margin-left:auto    }
H1  { border-left:2em     }
H1  { border-right:auto   }
```

Related Attributes...	Go to page...
border-left	36
border-right	38
margin-left	110
margin-right	112
padding-left	130
padding-right	132
width	173

ID as Selector

Syntax

```
#z086y ( ...: ... }
```

Definition

Using the ID as the selector allows the designer to take full advantage of CSS. The option to use ID selectors gives the user the ability to set style properties on each element.

Note that when you use an ID as the selector, you must use the HTML end tag (/). This is especially important to remember if you do not normally use the optional end tags.

Category

Basic concepts

Example Syntax

```
#a123b {font-size: 12pt}
<P ID=a123b>This paragraph is different from the
others.</p>
```

Related Topics...	Go to page...
fonts	69
H1-H6	81
Lists	100
P	126

IMG

Syntax

```
IMG { ... : ... }
```

Definition

Using style sheets, you can take advantage of other CSS properties to dynamically alter the way an image is displayed on your Web site.

With CSS, you can manipulate your image by creating different border styles, by adjusting its height and width, by determining its placement, by embedding it in the background of the body, or by setting float values.

IMG

Most of the restrictions you have grown accustomed to with HTML are now gone. It will take you some time to get comfortable using style sheets and a lot more work will be required to place your images in a document. However, if you take the time to use style sheets, you will be rewarded for your efforts with a great looking presentation.

Read all the related attributes; they provide important tips for correctly setting the properties of the image and they describe all the options available for placing your image.

Category

Links and graphics

Example Syntax

```
IMG.day {border-style: double}
```

Related Topics...	Go to page...
background	29
BODY	33
border	33
border-bottom	35
border-left	36
border-right	38
border-top	41
clear	49
float	68
height	82
margin	107
margin-bottom	109
margin-left	110
margin-right	112
margin-top	114

important

Syntax

... {...:... ! important }

Definition

Style sheets are meant to provide both the author and the user with greater control over the appearance of a site.

This is generally a good idea. However, sometimes there are style properties that you really want viewed exactly as you have designed them. Although the reader control feature is quite powerful, there is an override. By adding ! important to your code, the user style sheet is forced to accept your style attributes.

Don't go overboard with this function. Users will appreciate the option of being able to customize the site. If you plan properly, you can allow the modification of elements such as the background color and font size, but still maintain control over the appearance, giving the user the option to customize less important attributes.

Both user and author have access to the ! important rule. A user's ! important overrides an author normal rule, but an author ! important rule overrides a user ! important.

Category

Basic Concepts

important

Example Syntax

```
<p> {font: red ! important }
```

in

Syntax

```
...  {... : ...in  }
```

Definition

`in` equals inches and, being a unit of measurement, this value is commonly found in the `font-size`, `line-height`, `margin`, `padding`, `border`, `word-spacing`, etc.

`in` is an absolute value. 1 in.=2.54cm.

Category

Units

Example Syntax

```
H1 { line-height: 0.5in }
```

Related Attributes...	Go to page...
auto	28
cm	50
em	64
ex	66
mm	119
pc	135
pt	140
px	142

Inheritance

Syntax

```
...  { ...:... }    [1]
      ...  { ...:... }      [2]
```

Definition

The inheritance rules determine if an element is to inherit the properties of its parent element.

Refer to the table that follows the example syntax to determine if you are working with a property that inherits elements of the parent.

Category

Basic Concepts

Example Syntax

```
P {word-spacing: 0.2em}
```

Property	Inherits	Go to page...
A	✔	21
background		29
border		33
border-bottom		35
border-left		36
border-right		38
border-top		41
clear		49
color	✔	52
float		68

inset

Syntax

...   { border-style: inset }

Definition

A 3-D inset is drawn as the border, based on the color values set.

Category

Box Properties

Example Syntax

H1 {border-style: inset red }

Related Attributes...	Go to page...
dashed	59
dotted	62
double	63
groove	80
outset	124
ridge	146
solid	148

Related Topics...	Go to page...
BODY	33
border	33
border-bottom	35

italic

Syntax

… { font-style: italic }

Definition

In the browser Font database, all fonts that are normally known as italic, cursive, or kursiv will be labeled as italic.

If there are no italic fonts available in the font-family, the browser will select one labeled oblique. If there are none labeled italic or oblique, the browser will select and display the normal font for that font-family.

Category

Font

Example Syntax

```
H3 { font-style:italic }
```

Related Attributes...	Go to page...
normal	123
oblique	123

Related Topics...	Go to page...
font	69
font-family	70
font-size	74
font-style	77
font-variant	78
font-weight	79

Length Units

Syntax

```
... { ... : [cm] | [em] | [ex] | [in] | [mm] | [pc] | [pt] | [px] }
```

Definition

A length value is inserted into the code after `margin` or `font-size` or one of the other sizing properties. `Line-height` is also a length value.

Some properties such as `margins` allow a negative number as the length value. `Padding` explicitly prohibits negative values.

Category

Units

Example Syntax

```
H1 { border: 12pt}
```

Related Attributes...	Go to page...
cm	50
em	64
ex	66
mm	119
pc	135
pt	140
px	142

Related Topics...	Go to page...
border	33
border-bottom	35
border-left	36
border-right	38
border-top	41
font	69
font-size	74
height	82

continues

Length Units

continued

letter-spacing

Syntax

    ...   {letter-spacing: ... }

Definition

Change the default value of the letter spacing in any way you want. This property effects the visual presentation of your document. You can use negative numbers as well as positive numbers to give either more space or less between letters.

Category

Text

Example Syntax

H1 {letter-spacing: 3em}

Related Attributes...	Go to page...
cm	50
em	64
ex	66
mm	119
Negative values	121
normal	123
pc	135
pt	140
px	142

Related Topics...	Go to page...
letter-spacing	96
line-height	98
text-align	155
text-indent	158
text-transform	161
text-decoration	157
vertical-align	170
word-spacing	174

line-height

Syntax

```
... {line-height: ... }
```

Definition

`line-height` is the distance between the baselines of two lines.
Negative values are *not* allowed.

Category

Text

Example Syntax

```
P { line-height: 1.2; font-size: 8pt }
```

Related Attributes...	Go to page...
cm	50
em	64
ex	66
mm	119
pc	135
pt	140
px	142

Related Topics...	Go to page...
font	69
font-size	74
Negative values	121

LINK

Syntax

```
A:LINK { …:… }
```

Definition

Links are pointers to other spots in the same document or to other documents that are part of the same Web, or are references to other WWW documents—truly the most amazing aspect of the World Wide Web.

Category

Links and Graphics

Example Syntax

```
A:link   { text-decoration:none;
              color:blue;
              font-size: 10pt;
              font-weight: bold
         }     /*  Unvisited link information is
set as stated  */

A:visited   { color:#00009c; text-decoration:line-
              through;
              font-size: 8pt;
              font-weight: bold
         }     /*  Visited link will have a strike
through  */
-- >
</STYLE>
</HEAD>
<BODY>
<p>
<center>
<h6>LINKS</h6>
  <a href="http://www.hwg.org">HTML Writers Guild
➥</A> {HWG} <br>
```

Link

```
  <a href="http://www.w3.org">W3C</A> <br>
  <a href="http://www.cwebdev.com">Crystal Web
➥Designs</A> <br>
  <a href="http://www.netroute.net">Canadian
➥ISP</A><br>
<a href="www.que.mcp.com">www.que.mcp.com</a> <br>
<a href="www.ladydars.com">www.ladydars.com</a>
</center>
</p>
```

Fig. 6. Links using Cascading Style Sheets

Lists

Syntax

... {   ...:...   }

Definition

Style sheets make lists more attractive by adding more list styles. Using style sheets, you can attach a label to list-items. The label will be placed outside of the content and will be rendered based on the properties of the element to which it is attached.

Category

Lists

Example Syntax

```
UL {background:gold;
        list-style:none;
        font:16px fantasy;
        color:#424263    }
UL LI { border:dashed thick green;
        margin:3px;
        padding:1px;
        font:15px Western   }
UL LI LI {    font: 12px          }
OL  {background:yellow; list-style:roman;
        font: 18px Western;
        color:#424263
        }
OL LI LI { font-size:12px}
OL LI LI LI {font:10px courier new}
-- >
</STYLE>
</HEAD>
<BODY>
<p>
<ul>best viewed with<br><li>MSIE 3<UL><LI> beta 2
or higher</li></UL></LI><li>----</li></ul>  As new
commercial CSS compliant browsers become available
they will be added to the list.
</p>
<hr>
```

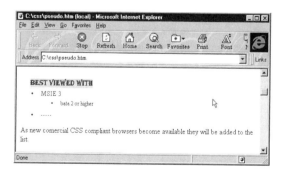

Fig. 7. Lists also benefit from CSS.

Lists

Related Attributes...	Go to page...
circle	47
decimal	60
disc	61
lower-alpha	105
lower-roman	106
none	122
square	151
upper-alpha	167
upper-roman	168

Related Topics...	Go to page...
border	33
border-bottom	35
border-left	36
border-right	38
border-top	41
list-style	102

list-style

Syntax

```
...   { list-style: <keyword> || <position> || <url>...}
...   { list-style:[disc]|[circle]|[square]|[decimal]|
```

```
[lower-roman]|[upper-roman]|[lower-alpha]|
[upper-alpha]|[none]
   || [inside]|[outside]  ||  [URL] }
```

Definition

There are nine list styles from which to choose. You may also choose to place the list marker inside or outside. If no selection is made, disc outside is the default display value for placement. The list-style property can be placed on any element in the style sheet. The properties set will be inherited to any child element. The list-style properties will only be displayed through elements with the display value list-item or <LI>.

Category

List

Example Syntax

UL UL {list-style: square outside }

Related Attributes...	Go to page...
circle	47
decimal	60
disc	61
lower-alpha	105
lower-roman	106
none	122
square	151
upper-alpha	167
upper-roman	168

lowercase

Syntax

... {text-transform: lowercase }

Definition

Selecting the lowercase attribute causes all the letters in the element to be displayed as lowercase.

Category

Text

Example Syntax

H3 { text-transform: lowercase }

Related Attributes...	Go to page...
capitalize	46
none	122
uppercase	169

Related Topics...	Go to page...
letter-spacing	96
line-height	98
text-align	155
text-indent	158
text-transform	161
text-decoration	170
vertical-align	170
word-spacing	174

lower-alpha

Syntax

... { list-style:lower-alpha }

Definition

The lower-alpha attribute displays lower alpha characters to mark the list items. There are several other styles available.

Category

List

Example Syntax

UL { list-style:lower-alpha }

Related Attributes...	Go to page...
circle	47
decimal	60
disc	61
lower-roman	106
none	122
square	151
upper-alpha	167
upper-roman	168

Related Topics...	Go to page...
list-style	102

lower-roman

Syntax

... { list-style:lower-roman }

Definition

The lower-roman attribute displays lower roman characters to mark the list items. There are several other styles available.

Category

List

Example Syntax

UL { list-style:lower-roman }

Related Attributes...	Go to page...
circle	47
decimal	60
disc	61
lower-alpha	105
none	122
square	151
upper-alpha	167
upper-roman	168

Related Topics...	Go to page...
list-style	102

margin

Syntax

```
... { margin: ... }
```

Definition

The `margin` property, which is a combination of `margin-top`, `margin-bottom`, `margin-left`, and `margin-right`, sets the outer edge of the element.

When you apply margin properties to replaced elements, you are telling the browser what is the minimal distance from the replaced element to the rest of the content of the element.

It is possible to express only the one value `margin`. If, however, you choose to set two or three values, the unwritten values will be taken from the opposite sides.

Category

Box Properties

Example Syntax

```
BODY { margin: 1.2em }
```

Related Attributes...	Go to page...
auto	28
cm	50
em	64
ex	66
length (*units*)	94

continues

margin

continued

Related Attributes...	Go to page...
mm	119
pc	135
pt	140
px	142

Related Topics...	Go to page...
border	33
border-bottom	35
border-left	36
border-right	38
border-top	41
clear	49
float	68
height	82
margin-bottom	109
margin-left	110
margin-right	112
margin-top	114
padding	127
padding-bottom	129
padding-left	130
padding-right	132
padding-top	134
width	173

margin-bottom

Syntax

```
... { margin-bottom: ... }
```

Definition

To specify the bottom margin for the element as anything other than equal to the other three sides, you use this property. *Remember, you can set the margin for the entire element with* margin.

Category

Box Properties

Example Syntax

```
H3 { margin-bottom: 3em }
```

Related Attributes...	Go to page...
auto	28
cm	50
em	64
ex	66
length (*units*)	94
mm	119
pc	135
pt	140
px	142

margin-bottom

margin-left

Syntax

```
… { margin-left: … }
```

Definition

In some situations, you may want to use different margin sizes. You use the `margin-left` property to specify the left margin. *Remember, you can set the margin for the entire element with one word,* `margin`.

Category

Box Properties

Example Syntax

```
BODY { margin-left: 2em }
```

Related Attributes...	Go to page...
auto	28
cm	50
em	64
ex	66
length(*units*)	94
mm	119
pc	135
pt	140
px	142

Related Topics...	Go to page...
border	33
border-bottom	35

continues

margin-left

continued

margin-right

Syntax

... { margin-right: ... }

Definition

The right margin for the element is set with the margin-right prop-erty. *Remember, you can set the margin for the entire element with one word,* margin.

Category

Box Properties

Example Syntax

```
H1 { margin-right: 1.2em }
```

Related Attributes...	Go to page...
auto	28
cm	50
em	64
ex	66
length (*units*)	94
mm	119
pc	135
pt	140
px	142

Related Topics...	Go to page...
border	33
border-bottom	35
border-left	36
border-right	38
border-top	41
clear	49
float	68
height	82

continues

margin-right

continued

margin-top

Syntax

... { margin-top: ... }

Definition

The top margin for the element is set using the margin-top property. *Remember, you can set the margin for the entire element with one word*, margin.

Category

Box Properties

Example Syntax

```
IMG { margin-top: auto }
```

Related Attributes...	Go to page...
auto	28
cm	50
em	64
ex	66
length (*units*)	94
mm	119
pc	135
pt	140
px	142

Related Topics...	Go to page...
border	33
border-bottom	35
border-left	36
border-right	38
border-top	41
clear	49
float	68
height	82

continues

margin-top

---

continued

Related Topics...	Go to page...
margin	107
margin-bottom	109
margin-left	110
margin-right	114
padding	127
padding-bottom	129
padding-left	130
padding-right	132
padding-top	134
width	173

---

medium

Syntax

... {border: ...   medium ...   }

Definition

medium is an attribute that represents the width of the border and is also the default setting. Other attributes are thick and thin.

Category

Box Properties

Example Syntax

H1 {border: solid medium blue}

Related Attributes...	Go to page...
thick	162
thin	164

Related Topics...	Go to page...
border	33
border-bottom	35
border-left	36
border-right	38
border-top	41
clear	49
float	68
height	82
margin	107
margin-bottom	109
margin-left	110
margin-right	112
margin-top	114
padding	127
padding-bottom	129
padding-left	130
padding-right	132
padding-top	134
width	173

middle

Syntax

... {vertical-align: middle }

Definition

middle will align an image with the vertical midpoint of the baseline plus half the x-height.

Category

Text

Example Syntax

IMG {vertical-align: middle }

Related Attributes...	Go to page...
baseline	31
sub	152
super	154
top	165

Related Topics...	Go to page...
letter-spacing	96
line-height	98
text-align	155
text-top	160
text-decoration	157
text-indent	158

mm

Syntax

... { ... : ...mm }

Definition

The mm unit defines sizable properties in millimeters.

Category

Unit

Example Syntax

H1 { border: 1mm }

Related Attributes...	Go to page...
auto	28
cm	50
em	64
ex	66
pc	135
pt	140
px	142

mm

Related Topics...	Go to page...
border	33
border-bottom	35
border-left	36
border-right	38
border-top	41
font	69
font-size	74
height	82
letter-spacing	96
line-height	98
margin	107
margin-bottom	109
margin-left	110
margin-right	112
margin-top	114
padding	127
padding-bottom	129
padding-left	130
padding-right	132
padding-top	134
text-indent	158
width	173
word-spacing	174

Negative Values

Syntax

... { ...: -...em }

Definition

Negative values are permitted under certain circumstances. Implementing some negative values can be problematic.

For a complete list of properties that support negative values (in theory) see the "Related Attributes" table.

Category

Units

Example Syntax

H1 {margin-right: -0.5mm}

Related Attributes...	Go to page...
background	29
letter-spacing	96
margin	107
margin-bottom	109
margin-left	110
margin-right	112
margin-top	114
text-indent	158
word spacing	174

Related Topics...	Go to page...
Length Units	94

none

Syntax

... { ...:none }

Definition

The attribute none can be applied to many of the properties. In each case, it effects the display of that property. In most cases, it neutralizes the property so that you don't see anything you would relate with the property.

It is useful with a property like list-style in that it allows you to choose no marker as the list-item marker. In other cases, it is useful because it allows you to set exceptions to the general rule of that property.

Category

All

Example Syntax

H1.plain { text-decoration: none }

Related Attributes...	Go to page...
border-style	39
clear	49
float	68
list-style	102
text-decoration	157
text-transform	161

normal

Syntax

… { …:normal }

Definition

normal, in most cases, tells the browser to format this element with the normal settings for the associated property.

It can also be used to make exceptions to a set of defined property styles. For example, if you set the H1 properties with a font-style of italic, you may redefine the settings for one occurrence, or for a class of the element that is to be formatted as normal by the browser.

Category

All

Example Syntax

H1.abc {font-style:normal}

Related Attributes...	Go to page...
font-style	77
font-variant	78
font-weight	79
letter-spacing	96
white-space	173
word-spacing	174

oblique

Syntax

… {font-style:oblique}

Definition

`oblique` fonts are fonts that are commonly known as oblique, slanted, or incline.

If the browser can't find a font called `oblique` in the chosen font-family, it should slant the normal font to create the desired effect.

Category

Font

Example Syntax

```
H3 { font-style:oblique }
```

Related Attributes...	Go to page...
italic	93
normal	123

Related Topics...	Go to page...
font	69
font-size	74
font-style	77
letter-spacing	96
text-indent	158
word-spacing	174

outset

Syntax

```
... { border-style: outset }
```

Definition

A 3-D `outset` is drawn as the border, based on the color values set.

Category

Box Properties

Example Syntax

`H2 { border-style:outset }`

Related Attributes...	Go to page...
dashed	59
dotted	62
double	63
groove	80
inset	92
ridge	146
solid	148

Related Topics...	Go to page...
background	29
BODY	33
border	33
border-bottom	35
border-left	36
border-right	38
border-top	41
clear	49

continues

continued

P

Syntax

P { ...:... }

Definition

In HTML, P tells the browser to make a new paragraph. It formats a BR before and after the P, making it a block-level element.

In CSS, P is used to define what the HTML <P> element will look like. You can also specify classes of P to make exceptions to the general P rules you specify.

Category

All

Example Syntax

`P {font-size: 12pt }`

padding

Syntax

`… { …:… ; padding: … }`

Definition

`Padding`, which is made up of `padding-left`, `padding-right`, `padding-top`, and `padding-bottom`, tells the browser how much space to put between the border and the image or text of the element.

Category

Box Properties

Example Syntax

`H1 { background:transparent ; padding: 1.2em }`

Related Attributes...	Go to page...
auto	28
cm	50
em	64
ex	66
mm	119

continues

padding

continued

Related Attributes...	Go to page...
length (*units*)	94
pc	135
pt	140
px	142

Related Topics...	Go to page...
border	33
border-bottom	35
border-left	36
border-right	38
border-top	41
margin	107
margin-bottom	109
margin-left	110
margin-right	112
margin-top	114
padding-bottom	129
padding-left	130
padding-right	132
padding-top	134

padding-bottom

Syntax

... { ...:... ; padding-bottom: ... }

Definition

padding-bottom tells the browser how much space there is between the image or text and the bottom border.

Category

Box Properties

Example Syntax

H1 { background:transparent ; padding-bottom:
➥1.2em }

Related Attributes...	Go to page...
auto	28
cm	50
em	64
ex	66
length (units)	94
mm	119
pc	135
pt	140
px	142

padding-bottom

padding-left

Syntax

... { ...:... ; padding-left: ... }

Definition

The space between the border and the text or image on the left side is set with padding-left.

Category

Box Properties

Example Syntax

```
H1 { background:transparent ; padding-left: 1.2em }
```

Related Attributes...	Go to page...
auto	28
cm	50
em	64
ex	66
in	xxx
length (units)	94
mm	119
pc	135
pt	140
px	142

Related Topics...	Go to page...
border	33
border-bottom	35
border-left	36
border-right	38
border-top	41
margin	107
margin-bottom	109

continues

padding-left

continued

Related Topics...	Go to page...
margin-left	110
margin-right	112
margin-top	114
padding	127
padding-bottom	129
padding-right	132
padding-top	134

padding-right

Syntax

... { ...:... ; padding-right: ... }

Definition

The space between the border and the text or image on the right side is set with padding-right.

Category

Box Properties

Example Syntax

H1 { background:transparent ; padding-right:
➥1.2em }

Related Attributes...	Go to page...
auto	28
cm	50

em	64
ex	66
length (*units*)	94
mm	119
pc	135
pt	140
px	142

padding-top

Syntax

```
... { ...:... ; padding-top: ... }
```

Definition

To set the padding for the top of your text or image (element), use `padding-top`.

Category

Box Properties

Example Syntax

```
H1 { background:transparent ; padding-top: 1.2em }
```

Related Attributes...	Go to page...
auto	28
cm	50
em	64
ex	66
length (units)	94
mm	119
pc	135
pt	140
px	142

pc

Syntax

... { ...: 1pc }

Definition

pc picas=12 points (12pt). Used for determining sizing of sizable properties.

Category

Units

Example Syntax

```
H3 {font-size:1.2pc}
```

Related Attributes...	Go to page...
auto	28
cm	50
em	64
ex	66
length (units)	94
mm	119
pt	140
px	142

Related Topics...	Go to page...
border	33
border-bottom	35
border-left	36
border-right	38
border-top	41
font	69
font-size	74
height	82
letter-spacing	96
line-height	98
margin	107
margin-bottom	109

Percentage Units

Syntax

... { ...:...% }

Definition

It is often better to express a length unit value as a percentage of the parent element rather than a whole value. The percentage value you express is taken as a percentage of the parent element.

By using a percentage, you will not end up with a font the size of an HTML H1 or H6 element when all you really want, for example, is a font that is half the size of the parent or a font that is one and a half times bigger than the parent element.

Category

Units

Example Syntax

```
H1 { line-height: 120% }
```

Percentage Units

Percentage values that can be used by...	Go to page...
background	29
font-size	74
line-height	98
margin	107
margin-bottom	109
margin-left	110
margin-right	112
margin-top	114
padding	127
padding-bottom	129
padding-left	130
padding-right	132
padding-top	134
text-indent	158
vertical-align	170
width	173

Related Topics...	Go to page...
auto	28
cm	50
em	64
ex	66
mm	119
pc	135

pt	140
px	142

Position

Syntax

```
BODY  { background: (url) top left }
```

Definition

Once you have chosen the background image, you have to decide where to position the image.

Category

Basic Concepts

Example Syntax

```
BODY { background: http://www.cwebdev.com/cwd.gif
➥0% 50% }
```

Key to positioning...	Percentages...	Keywords...
Top	0%	top
Center	50%	center
Bottom	100%	bottom
Left	0%	left
Right	100%	right
Upper-left	0% 0%	top left
Center top	0% 50%	top center

continues

Position

continued

Key to positioning...	Percentages...	Keywords...
Center left	50% 0%	center left
Center right	50% 100%	center right
Center bottom	100% 50%	bottom center
Bottom left	100% 0%	bottom left
Bottom right	100% 100%	bottom right

Related Topics...	Go to page...
background	29
BODY	33
color	52
repeat	144
scroll	147
transparent	166

pt

Syntax

...{ ...: ...pt }

Definition

pt (points); 1 pt=1/72 in. Points are used for determining sizing of sizable properties. Points represent an absolute value, inches, expressed as a fraction.

Category

Units

Example Syntax

H3 {font-size:15pt}

Related Attributes...	Go to page...
auto	28
cm	50
em	64
ex	66
length (*units*)	94
mm	119
pc	135
px	142

Related Topics...	Go to page...
border	33
border-bottom	35
border-left	36
border-right	38
border-top	41

continues

pt

continued

Related Topics...	Go to page...
font	69
font-size	74
height	82
letter-spacing	96
line-height	98
margin	107
margin-bottom	109
margin-left	110
margin-right	112
margin-top	114
padding	127
padding-bottom	129
padding-left	130
padding-right	132
padding-top	134
text-indent	158
width	173
word-spacing	174

px

Syntax

```
...{ ...: ...px }
```

Definition

px (pixels)=relative to canvas size. Pixels are used for determining sizing of sizable properties. This is a relative value.

Category

Units

Example Syntax

H3 {font-size:1.2px}

Related Attributes...	Go to page...
auto	28
cm	50
em	64
ex	66
length (units)	94
mm	119
pc	135
pt	140

Related Topics...	Go to page...
border	33
border-bottom	35
border-left	36
border-right	38
border-top	41
font	69

continues

continued

repeat

Syntax

```
BODY { background: (url) repeat }
```

Definition

The best way to understand the use of repeat is to understand that it performs the same job as `<background="*.gif>`, which repeats the image over and over on the background of the Web page.

There are other ways to determine the repeat value. For example, `repeat-x` tells the browser to repeat the image horizontally across the entire page. `repeat-y` provides a vertical repeat of the image. `no-repeat` does exactly what you think; it tells the browser to not repeat the image.

The default value is repeat, so if you want the image to appear a certain way in the background, you need to set the repeat values appropriately.

Related Attributes...	Action...
repeat	covers canvas
repeat-y	repeats vertically
repeat-x	repeats horizontally
no-repeat	does not repeat

Category

Color and Background

Example Syntax

```
BODY  { background: (url) repeat }
```

Related Topics...	Go to page...
background	29
BODY	33

continues

repeat

continued

Related Topics...	Go to page...
color	52
repeat	144
scroll	147
transparent	166

ridge

Syntax

... { border-style: ridge }

Definition

A 3-D ridge is drawn as the border, based on the color values set.

Category

Box Properties

Example Syntax

H2 { border-style: ridge }

Related Attributes...	Go to page...
dashed	59
dotted	62
double	63
groove	80
inset	92
outset	124
solid	148

scroll

Syntax

```
... { background: (url) ... ...  [scroll]|[fixed] }
```

Definition

With scroll, your background image will scroll with the user. I like to use scroll, which happens to be the default setting.

Category

Color and Background

Example Syntax

```
BODY  { background:  (url)  repeat }
```

Related Attributes...	Go to page...
BODY	23
background	29
color	52
repeat	144
transparent	166

solid

Syntax

```
...  { border-style: solid }
```

Definition

A solid border, based on the color values set, is drawn around the element.

Category

Box Properties

Example Syntax

```
H2 { border-style: solid }
```

Related Attributes...	Go to page...
dashed	59
dotted	62
double	63
groove	80
inset	92
outset	124
ridge	146

Related Topics...	Go to page...
background	29
BODY	33
border	33
border-bottom	35
border-left	36
border-right	38
border-top	41
float	68
height	82
margin	107
margin-bottom	109
margin-left	110
margin-right	112

continues

solid

continued

Related Topics...	Go to page...
margin-top	114
padding	127
padding-bottom	129
padding-left	130
padding-right	132
padding-top	134
width	173

SPAN

Syntax

`<SPAN STYLE="...:...; ...:...">` text here `</SPAN>`

Definition

The SPAN element provides for in-line style. SPAN can be used very effectively to modify the appearance of a section on one page, while the rest of the style settings continue to rely on the style layout in the style sheet.

Concern has been expressed that designers will skip the style sheet and rely solely on in-line style. This would be a mistake for any designer as it would entail a lot more typing than is necessary when using the style sheet or using HTML alone.

Category

Basic Concepts

Example Syntax

```
<SPAN STYLE="color:green; border: solid blue>
```

square

Syntax

```
... { list-style:square }
```

Definition

The list marker display is a square. There are several other styles available.

Category

List

Example Syntax

```
UL { list-style:square }
```

Related Attributes...	Go to page...
circle	47
decimal	60
disc	61
lower-alpha	105
lower-roman	106
none	122
upper-alpha	167
upper-roman	168

STYLE

Syntax

```
< STYLE TYPE="text/css" >
```

Definition

The <STYLE> tag is used to create style sheets in the
<HEAD></HEAD> of an HTML document. Examples of
each implementation of the style sheets can be found in
the indexes.

Category

Basic Concepts

Example Syntax

```
< STYLE TYPE="text/css" >
```

Related Topics...	Go to page...
SPAN	xxx
<!—	xxx

sub

Syntax

```
... {vertical-align: sub }
```

Definition

sub (subscript) can be used in an HTML document by using this CSS
attribute. This is one of the many improvements to the Web that will
give it a more professional appearance.

Category

Text

Example Syntax

```
SUB {vertical-align: sub }
 /*class name  (SUB)  is used so this can */
/* be used anywhere in the document */
<P>Try placing a <B class="SUB">subscript</B>
➥anywhere you wish.</P>
```

Related Attributes...	Go to page...
baseline	31
middle	118
super	154
top	165

Related Topics...	Go to page...
letter-spacing	96
line-height	98
text-align	155
text-bottom	156
text-decoration	157
text-indent	158
text-top	160
text-transform	161
vertical-align	170
word-spacing	174

super

Syntax

... {vertical-align: super }

Definition

super=superscript; CSS enables you to include superscript in your Web document. The following example shows how to implement superscript into your HTML document.

Category

Text

Example Syntax

SUPER {vertical-align: super }
/* The class name SUPER is used */

Related Attributes...	Go to page...
baseline	31
middle	118
sub	152
top	165

Related Topics...	Go to page...
letter-spacing	96
line-height	98
text-align	155

text-align

Syntax

```
...  { text-align: ...  }
```

Definition

text-align tells the browser how to align the text within the element. The alignment will effect the text within the element only, as opposed to an HTML align=center (for example), which would center the entire element across the canvas. text-align can be used with left, right, center, and justify.

Category

Text

Example Syntax

```
...  { text-align:center }
```

text-bottom

Syntax

... {vertical-align: text-bottom }

Definition

text-bottom aligns the bottom of the text with the bottom of the
parent element.

Category

Text

Example Syntax

... {vertical-align: text-bottom }

sub	152
top	165

text-decoration

Syntax

```
...  {  text-decoration: [none]|[underline]|
[overline]|[line-through]|[blink]  }
```

Definition

As its name suggests, text-decoration adds decoration to your text. There will be many additions to this particular property in the future.

This property has no effect on empty elements or on non-text elements such as images.

Category

Text

Example Syntax

```
H3 { text-decoration: line-through }
```

Related Attributes...

```
blink

line-through

none

overline

underline
```

text-indent

Syntax

```
... {text-indent: ... }
```

Definition

`text-indent` can be used to place an indent at the beginning of a paragraph. You must use the `</P>` tag at the end of the paragraph. Otherwise, the browser will not consider the next `<P>` tag to be valid for indenting purposes. `text-indent` can only be used *once* in any paragraph.

It is possible to have a negative indent. Not all browsers will support negative indents. `Indent` can be set as a percentage of the parent element, i.e., `<P>`.

Category

Text

Example Syntax

```
.oct  {font:50px fantasy;
          margin-bottom:-20px; }
.test  {font-size:160%;
          margin-bottom:-6px;
          margin-top:-6px;
       text-indent:15px}
.scaps  {font-size:60%;  margin-bottom:6px}
-->
</STYLE>
</HEAD>
<BODY>
<center>
<B class="oct">The October Comet</B><!-- Copyright
➥(C)1996 James R. Falla -->
</center>
<p>
<b class="test">A</B><b class="scaps">ALL EYES
LOOKED TO THE SKY</b> as an enormous comet hurtled
to the earth leaving an eerie green trail in its
wake.  It appeared to those watching that the comet
slammed down just beyond the town to the east.
Within minutes a parade of cars, trucks and
bicycles were heading down Deer Park Rd. towards
the imagined crash site.  </p>
```

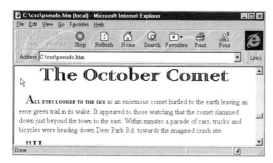

Fig. 8. Indented text is achieved by using `text-indent`.

Related Attributes...	Go to page...
cm	50
em	64
ex	66
mm	119
pc	135
pt	140
px	142

text-top

Syntax

```
... {vertical-align: text-top }
```

Definition

text-top aligns the top of the text with the top of the parent element.

Category

Text

Example Syntax

```
TA {vertical-align: text-top } /*class name TA*/
```

Related Attributes...	Go to page...
baseline	31
middle	118

text-transform

Syntax

... {text-transform:... }

Definition

text-transform provides the choice of capitalizing the first letter of each word with capitalize, capitalizing all text in the element with uppercase, lowercasing the entire element with lowercase, or ignoring inherited properties with none.

text-transform

Category

Text

Example Syntax

`H1 { text-transform:capitalize }`

Related Attributes...	Go to page...
capitalize	46
lowercase	104
none	122
uppercase	169

Related Topics...	Go to page...
letter-spacing	96
line-height	98
text-align	155
text-decoration	157
text-indent	158
vertical-align	170
word-spacing	174

thick

Syntax

`... {border: ... thick ... }`

Definition

thick is an attribute that is used to express the width of the border.

Category

Box Properties

Example Syntax

```
...  {border: ...  thick  ...  }
```

Related Attributes...	Go to page...
medium	116
thin	164

Related Topics...	Go to page...
border	33
border-bottom	35
border-left	36
border-right	38
border-top	41
margin	107
margin-bottom	109
margin-left	110
margin-right	112
margin-top	114
padding	127
padding-bottom	129
padding-left	130
padding-right	132
padding-top	134

thin

Syntax

```
...  {border: ...  thin  ...  }
```

Definition

`thin` is another attribute that is used to express the width of the border.

Category

Box Properties

Example Syntax

```
IMG  {border: solid  thin  red  }
```

Related Attributes...	Go to page...
medium	116
thick	164

Related Topics...	Go to page...
border	33
border-bottom	35
border-left	36
border-right	38
border-top	41
margin	107
margin-bottom	109
margin-left	110

top

Syntax

...   {Vertical-align: top }

Definition

The vertical-align attribute top forces the element to align with the tallest element on the line.

Category

Text

Example Syntax

H1 {vertical-align: top }

Related Attributes...	Go to page...
baseline	31
middle	118

continues

continued

Related Attributes...	Go to page...
sub	152
super	154

Related Topics...	Go to page...
letter-spacing	96
line-height	98
text-align	155
text-bottom	156
text-decoration	157
text-indent	158
text-top	160
text-transform	161
vertical-align	170
word-spacing	174

transparent

Syntax

... {background: transparent }

Definition

The initial background setting is transparent. If you specify a color, transparent is overridden. However, when you do specify a color, transparent is still the default and the specified color is painted over the canvas.

If you specify that an image be included in the background, but you do not specify a background color, transparent regions of the image will be displayed as transparent. If there is a background color specified, the transparent regions of the image will be displayed in that background color.

Category

Images and Backgrounds

Example Syntax

```
BODY   {background: transparent }
or
TABLE  {background: transparent }
```

Related Attributes...	Go to page...
color	52
Position	139
repeat	144
scroll	147

Related Topics...	Go to page...
background	29
BODY	33

upper-alpha

Syntax

```
...  { list-style:upper-alpha  }
```

Definition

The list marker display attribute of `upper-alpha` will mark a list with uppercase alpha characters. There are several other styles available.

Category

List

Example Syntax

```
UL  { list-style:upper-alpha  }
```

Related Attributes...	Go to page...
circle	47
decimal	60
disc	61
lower-alpha	105
lower-roman	106
none	122
square	151
upper-roman	168

upper-roman

Syntax

```
...  { list-style:upper-roman  }
```

Definition

The `list-style` attribute `upper-roman` displays uppercase roman numerals as the list marker. There are several other styles available.

Category

List

Example Syntax

`UL  { list-style: upper-roman}`

Related Attributes...	Go to page...
circle	47
decimal	60
disc	61
lower-alpha	105
none	122
square	151
upper-alpha	167

uppercase

Syntax

`... { text-transform: uppercase }`

Definition

`uppercase` tells the browser to display all the letters of the element in uppercase.

Category

Text

Example Syntax

```
H3 { text-transform: uppercase }
```

Related Attributes...	Go to page...
capitalize	46
lowercase	104
none	122

Related Topics...	Go to page...
letter-spacing	96
line-height	98
text-align	155
text-decoration	157
text-indent	158
text-transform	161
vertical-align	170
word-spacing	174

vertical-align

Syntax

```
... {vertical-align:... }
```

Definition

The vertical-align property is used to determine the vertical positioning of the element.

There are many options available. Proper use of this property will result in some really good Web presentations.

Category

Text

Example Syntax

B {vertical-align: top }

Related Attributes...	Go to page...
baseline	31
middle	118
sub	152
super	154
top	165

Related Topics...	Go to page...
letter-spacing	96
line-height	98
text-align	155
text-bottom	156
text-decoration	157
text-indent	158
text-top	160
text-transform	161
word-spacing	174

VISITED

Syntax

```
A:VISITED {  ...:...  }
```

Definition

After a hypertext link has been visited, the browser typically changes the color to indicate that it has been visited. You can also change other attributes by making the visited links smaller or larger than the not-yet-visited links.

Category

Links and Graphics

Example Syntax

```
A:VISITED {  text-decoration:line-through  }
```

Related Attributes...	Go to page...
A	21
active	26
LINK	99

Related Topics...	Go to page...
Anchor Pseudo-classes	27
BODY	33
color	52
Font	69
IMG	85
Text	15
text-decoration	157

white-space

Syntax

... {white-space: [normal]|[pre]|[nowrap] }

Definition

This property tells the browser how to display white space within the element. white-space only applies to block level elements.

Related Attributes...	What it does...
normal	displays normal white space
nowrap	wrapping with only
pre	same as <PRE> in HTML

Category

Fonts

Example Syntax

...P.WS {white-space:nowrap } /*paragraph class WS*/

width

Syntax

... {width:...}

Definition

The most common use for width is for re-sizing in-line images. This property can be used only with block level and replaced elements. (Replaced elements are images.)

width

Category

Box Properties

Example Syntax

... {width:...}

Related Attributes...	Go to page...
margin	107
margin-bottom	109
margin-left	110
margin-right	112
margin-top	114
padding	127
padding-bottom	129
padding-left	130
padding-right	132
padding-top	134

word-spacing

Syntax

... { word-spacing: ... }

Definition

This property is used to change the default space between words. You can set the length value or, if you wish to make an exception to a general rule (element defined), you can use the normal setting.

This property can be applied to all elements (textual).

Category

Text

Example Syntax

`H2  {word-spacing:0.5em}`

Related Attributes...	Go to page...
cm	50
em	64
ex	66
mm	119
pc	135
pt	140
px	142

Related Topics...	Go to page...
letter-spacing	96
line-height	98
text-align	155
text-decoration	157
text-indent	158
text-transform	161
vertical-align	170

STYLE SHEETS IN ACTION

The following example has been tested on Microsoft Internet Explorer 3.1. Be sure to refer to the Quick Reference Section, as needed, while developing your own style sheets.

```
<!-- THIS IS A SAMPLE STYLE SHEET-->
<HTML>
<HEAD>

<STYLE  TYPE="text/css">
<!--

BODY       { background:white;
                   color:black
                   font-size:15px
}                   /*  The background is set as
is the color of text that is not tagged.  */


P   {margin-top=-1px;
      color:#00009c;
      font:16px, serif
  }                       /*  text color and font
data  */

/*  ------- links -------------------- next    -
------------------------------- */

A:link  { text-decoration:none;
           color:blue;
           font-size: 10pt;
           font-weight: bold
         }     /*  Unvisited link information is
```

Style Sheets in Action

```
    set    */

    A:visited    { color:#00009c; text-decoration:
    ➡line-through;
                            font-size: 8pt;
            font-weight: bold
                }    /*  Visited link information is
    set    */

    /*  ------- table --------------------- next    -
    ------------------------------ */

    TABLE    {background:yellow;
                        color:blue;
                        border:dashed thick green
                            }


    /*  ------- headings --------------------- next
    ------------------------------ */

    H1 {font:30px Courier new}
    H2 {font:30px Courier}
    H3  {font:30px fantasy }

    H4  {font:30px Western}
    H5  {font:30px Helvetica}
    H6  {font:30px Impact}

    /*  ----------- lists ------------ next    -----
    --------------------------- */

    UL {background:gold;  list-style:none;
            font:16px fantasy;
            color:#424263
            }

    UL LI { border:dashed thick green; margin:3px;
    ➡padding:1px;  font:15px Western  }
```

```
UL LI LI {    font: 12px         }

OL  {background:yellow; list-style:roman;
        font: 18px Western;
        color:#424263
        }

OL LI LI { font-size:12px}

OL LI LI LI {font:10px courier new}

/* ------- classes -------------------- next
------------------------------- */

.oct  {font:50px fantasy;
          margin-bottom:-20px; }
.test  {font-size:160%;
          margin-bottom:-6px;
          margin-top:-6px;
      text-indent:15px}
.scaps  {font-size:60%;  margin-bottom:6px}

.large{font-size:130%}
.supp{font-size:60%}


/* -------------- HTML ------------ next     ----
---------------------------- */



-->
</STYLE>


</HEAD>

<BODY >

<center>
<h6>Welcome to CSS </h6>
</center>
```

Style Sheets in Action

```
<p><b class="test">T</b>here are many aspects of
this new language that must be understood before it
can be applied.  If you have purchased a CSS how-to
book, like the companion book to this site<b> QUE'S
<u> HTML CSS Quick Reference</u> By James R. Falla
ISBN 0-7897-0135-8</b> you are well on your way to
mastering this language.</p>

<p><b class="test">A</b>s one of my editors re-
minded me, I promised to show examples of every CSS
property that would affect the appearance of the
document.  If I have missed anything, please feel
free to e-mail me at <A HREF="mailto:rfalla
➥@cwebdev.com">rfalla@cwebdev.com</A></p>

<p>
Bookmark Now!  Come back often, this site will be
updated to keep up with the new developments of
CSS1.
</p>
<hr>

<!-- --------------- LIST -------------- next
--------------------------------------- -->

<p>
<ul>best viewed with<br><li>MSIE 3<UL><LI> beta 2
or higher</li></UL></LI><li>—</li></ul>  As new
commercial CSS compliant browsers become available
they will be added to the list.
</p>
<hr>

<!-- -------------- Grouping --------------- next
--------------------------------------- -->

<ol><li>List item<ul><li>new font with drop
levels<ol><li>you can also use a different font-
family</li></ol></li><li>The more you put into
```

```
it<ol><li>The more you get out of it.</li>
➡</ol></li></ul></li><br>See for yourself<br><li>
➡second<ul><li>CSS EXTENSIBILITY</li><ol>
<li>Etc ...  (just try it!)</li></ol></ul>
➡</li><li>third</li><li>fourth</li></ol>
<hr>


<!-- --------------------------------------- next
---------------------------------------  -->


<h3>Introduction to CSS</h3>
<hr>


<!-- --------------- FONT ------------------- next
---------------------------------------  -->


<center>
<p>The following are examples of various fonts.
➡The font-size for each is 30px </p>
</center>
<table  border=1  width=100%>
<tr><td><center>
<H1>Courier new</H1>
</center></td>
<td><center>
<h2>Courier</h2>
</center></td></tr>
<tr><td><center>
<h3>Fantasy</h3>
</center></td>
<td><center>
<h4>Western</h4>
</center></td></tr>
<tr><td><center>
<h5>Helvetica</h5>
</center></td>
<td><center>
<h6>Impact</h6>
```

```
</center></td></tr>

</table><br><br>
<hr solid>

<!-- ---------- Class selector & Text Indent -------
next    ----------------------------------------
-->

<center>
<B class="oct">The October Comet</B><!- Copyright
➥(C)1996 James R. Falla ->
</center>

<p>
<b class="test">A</B><b class="scaps">LL EYES
LOOKED TO THE SKY</b> as an enormous comet hurtled
to the earth leaving an eerie green trail in its
wake.  It appeared to those watching that the comet
slammed down just beyond the town to the east.
Within minutes a parade of cars, trucks and bi-
cycles were heading down Deer Park Rd. towards the
imagined crash site.  </p>
<p>
<b class="test">"H</B>urry up Bill, if we can get
some comet fragments we can sell them to
collectors."<br>
"I've heard you can make a lot of money selling
comet fragments."<br>
"Only if we get there while there are pieces left
to get."
</p>
<p>
<b class="test">R</B>ick and Bill quickly packed a
few possible necessities in the pick-up truck.
They were sure they would need a shovel and a pick.
They choose to leave the wheel barrel.  They
quickly put the cap on the back of the truck, not
bothering to secure it, jumped in the truck and
```

```
headed for the comet.</p>

<hr>

<!--  --------------- Text-Decoration --------- next
-------------------------------------- -->

<p>
<center>
<h6>LINKS</h6>
  <a href="http://www.hwg.org">HTML Writers
➥Guild</A> {HWG} <br>
  <a href="http://www.w3.org">W3C</A> <br>
  <a href="http://www.cwebdev.com">Crystal Web
➥Designs</A> <br>
  <a href="http://www.netroute.net">Canadian
➥ISP</A><br>
➥<a href="http://www.que.mcp.com">www.que.mcp.com
➥</a> <br>
➥<a href="http://www.ladydars.com">
➥www.ladydars.com</a>

</center>
</p>
<hr>
<!--  ------------- Class as Selector ----- next
-------------------------------------- -->

<p>

It has been said that<b class="supp"> there are
no advantages</b> to having a web site on the
Internet.  The advantage is there, it's up to
the web developer to <b class="large">find and
exploit</b> the opportunities.
</p>

<p>
<b class="large">The thing to remember</b> when
designing your site is content is at least as
```

Style Sheets in Action

```
important as presentation style.  Use all the bells
and whistles you want, just make sure the site is
worth all the <b class="supp">HYPE</b>.
</p>

<p>

</p>

</BODY>
</HTML>
```

COLOR TABLES

These two color tables will help you find a color name by referencing the Hex/RGB Value or find the Hex/RGB Value when you reference the Color Name.

Proposed Color Codes Sorted by Color Name		Proposed Color Codes Sorted by Value	
Look Up the Color Name	Find the Value	Look Up the Value	Find the Color Name
Aquamarine	rgb=#70DB93	rgb=#23238E	Navy Blue
Baker's Chocolate	rgb=#5C3317	rgb=#236B8E	Steel Blue
Black	rgb=#000000	rgb=#215E21	Hunter Green
Blue	rgb=#0000FF	rgb=#007FFF	Slate Blue
Blue Violet	rgb=#9F5F9F	rgb=#238E23	Forest Green
Brass	rgb=#B5A642	rgb=#238E68	Sea Green
Bright Gold	rgb=#D9D919	rgb=#2F2F4F	Midnight Blue
Brown	rgb=#A62A2A	rgb=#2F4F2F	Dark Green
Bronze	rgb=#8C7853	rgb=#2F4F4F	Dark Slate Gray
Bronze II	rgb=#A67D3D	rgb=#3232CD	Medium Blue
Cadet Blue	rgb=#5F9F9F	rgb=#3299CC	Sky Blue
Cool Copper	rgb=#D98719	rgb=#32CD32	Lime Green
Copper	rgb=#B87333	rgb=#32CD99	Medium Aquamarine
Coral	rgb=#FF7F00	rgb=#38B0DE	Summer Sky
Corn Flower Blue	rgb=#42426F	rgb=#42426F	Corn Flower Blue
Cyan	rgb=#00FFFF	rgb=#00FF7F	Spring Green

continues

Color Tables

continued

Proposed Color Codes Sorted by Color Name		Proposed Color Codes Sorted by Value	
Look Up the Color Name	**Find the Value**	**Look Up the Value**	**Find the Color Name**
Dark Brown	rgb=#5C4033	rgb=#426F42	Medium Sea Green
Dark Green	rgb=#2F4F2F	rgb=#4A766E	Dark Green Copper
Dark Green Copper	rgb=#4A766E	rgb=#4D4DFF	Neon Blue
Dark Olive Green	rgb=#4F4F2F	rgb=#4E2F2F	Indian Red
Dark Orchid	rgb=#9932CD	rgb=#4F2F4F	Violet
Dark Purple	rgb=#871F78	rgb=#4F4F2F	Dark Olive Green
Dark Slate Blue	rgb=#6B238E	rgb=#527F76	Green Copper
Dark Slate Gray	rgb=#2F4F4F	rgb=#545454	Dim Gray
Dark Tan	rgb=#97694F	rgb=#5959AB	Rich Blue
Dark Turquoise	rgb=#7093DB	rgb=#5C3317	Baker's Chocolate
Dark Wood	rgb=#855E42	rgb=#5C4033	Dark Brown
Dim Gray	rgb=#545454	rgb=#5C4033	Very Dark Brown
Dusty Rose	rgb=#856363	rgb=#5F9F9F	Cadet Blue
Feldspar	rgb=#D19275	rgb=#6B238E	Dark Slate Blue
Firebrick	rgb=#8E2323	rgb=#6B4226	Semi-Sweet Chocolate
Forest Green	rgb=#238E23	rgb=#6B8E23	Medium Forest Green
Gold	rgb=#CD7F32	rgb=#6F4242	Salmon
Goldenrod	rgb=#DBDB70	rgb=#7093DB	Dark Turquoise
Gray	rgb=#C0C0C0	rgb=#70DB93	Aquamarine
Green	rgb=#00FF00	rgb=#0000FF	Blue
Green Copper	rgb=#527F76	rgb=#70DBDB	Medium Turquoise
Green Yellow	rgb=#93DB70	rgb=#7F00FF	Medium Slate Blue
Hunter Green	rgb=#215E21	rgb=#7FFF00	Medium Spring Green
Indian Red	rgb=#4E2F2F	rgb=#855E42	Dark Wood
Khaki	rgb=#9F9F5F	rgb=#856363	Dusty Rose

Color Tables

Proposed Color Codes Sorted by Color Name		Proposed Color Codes Sorted by Value	
Look Up the Color Name	Find the Value	Look Up the Value	Find the Color Name
Light Blue	rgb=#C0D9D9	rgb=#871F78	Dark Purple
Light Gray	rgb=#A8A8A8	rgb=#8C1717	Scarlet
Light Steel Blue	rgb=#8F8FBD	rgb=#8C7853	Bronze
Light Wood	rgb=#E9C2A6	rgb=#8E2323	Firebrick
Lime Green	rgb=#32CD32	rgb=#8E236B	Maroon
Magenta	rgb=#FF00FF	rgb=#00FF00	Green
Mandarin Orange	rgb=#E47833	rgb=#8E6B23	Sienna
Maroon	rgb=#8E236B	rgb=#8F8FBD	Light Steel Blue
Medium Aquamarine	rgb=#32CD99	rgb=#8FBC8F	Pale Green
Medium Blue	rgb=#3232CD	rgb=#9370DB	Medium Orchid
Medium Forest Green	rgb=#6B8E23	rgb=#93DB70	Green Yellow
Medium Goldenrod	rgb=#EAEAAE	rgb=#97694F	Dark Tan
Medium Orchid	rgb=#9370DB	rgb=#9932CD	Dark Orchid
Medium Sea Green	rgb=#426F42	rgb=#99CC32	Yellow Green
Medium Slate Blue	rgb=#7F00FF	rgb=#9F5F9F	Blue Violet
Medium Spring Green	rgb=#7FFF00	rgb=#9F9F5F	Khaki
Medium Turquoise	rgb=#70DBDB	rgb=#A62A2A	Brown
Medium Violet Red	rgb=#DB7093	rgb=#A67D3D	Bronze II
Medium Wood	rgb=#A68064	rgb=#A68064	Medium Wood
Midnight Blue	rgb=#2F2F4F	rgb=#A8A8A8	Light Gray
Navy Blue	rgb=#23238E	rgb=#ADEAEA	Turquoise
Neon Blue	rgb=#4D4DFF	rgb=#B5A642	Brass
Neon Pink	rgb=#FF6EC7	rgb=#B87333	Copper
New Midnight Blue	rgb=#00009C	rgb=#BC8F8F	Pink

continues

Color Tables

continued

Proposed Color Codes Sorted by Color Name		Proposed Color Codes Sorted by Value	
Look Up the Color Name	Find the Value	Look Up the Value	Find the Color Name
New Tan	rgb=#EBC79E	rgb=#C0C0C0	Gray
Old Gold	rgb=#CFB53B	rgb=#C0D9D9	Light Blue
Orange	rgb=#FF7F00	rgb=#CC3299	Violet Red
Orange Red	rgb=#FF2400	rgb=#CD7F32	Gold
Orchid	rgb=#DB70DB	rgb=#CDCDCD	Very Light Gray
Pale Green	rgb=#8FBC8F	rgb=#CFB53B	Old Gold
Pink	rgb=#BC8F8F	rgb=#D19275	Feldspar
Plum	rgb=#EAADEA	rgb=#D8BFD8	Thistle
Quartz	rgb=#D9D9F3	rgb=#D8D8BF	Wheat
Red	rgb=#FF0000	rgb=#00009C	New Midnight Blue
Rich Blue	rgb=#5959AB	rgb=#D98719	Cool Copper
Salmon	rgb=#6F4242	rgb=#D9D919	Bright Gold
Scarlet	rgb=#8C1717	rgb=#D9D9F3	Quartz
Sea Green	rgb=#238E68	rgb=#DB7093	Medium Violet Red
Semi-Sweet Chocolate	rgb=#6B4226	rgb=#DB70DB	Orchid
Sienna	rgb=#8E6B23	rgb=#DB9370	Tan
Silver	rgb=#E6E8FA	rgb=#DBDB70	Goldenrod
Sky Blue	rgb=#3299CC	rgb=#E47833	Mandarin Orange
Slate Blue	rgb=#007FFF	rgb=#E6E8FA	Silver
Spicy Pink	rgb=#FF1CAE	rgb=#E9C2A6	Light Wood
Spring Green	rgb=#00FF7F	rgb=#EAADEA	Plum
Steel Blue	rgb=#236B8E	rgb=#EAEAAE	Medium Goldenrod
Summer Sky	rgb=#38B0DE	rgb=#EBC79E	New Tan
Tan	rgb=#DB9370	rgb=#FF0000	Red

Color Tables

Proposed Color Codes Sorted by Color Name		Proposed Color Codes Sorted by Value	
Look Up the Color Name	Find the Value	Look Up the Value	Find the Color Name
Thistle	rgb=#D8BFD8	rgb=#FF00FF	Magenta
Turquoise	rgb=#ADEAEA	rgb=#FF1CAE	Spicy Pink
Very Dark Brown	rgb=#5C4033	rgb=#FF2400	Orange Red
Very Light Gray	rgb=#CDCDCD	rgb=#FF6EC7	Neon Pink
Violet	rgb=#4F2F4F	rgb=#FF7F00	Coral
Violet Red	rgb=#CC3299	rgb=#FF7F00	Orange
Wheat	rgb=#D8D8BF	rgb=#FFFF00	Yellow
White	rgb=#FFFFFF	rgb=#000000	Black
Yellow	rgb=#FFFF00	rgb=#00FFFF	Cyan
Yellow Green	rgb=#99CC32	rgb=#FFFFFF	White

GLOSSARY

The addition of Cascading Style Sheets (CSS) to the Internet brings with it some new terms and technical jargon for Internet users. This glossary will familiarize Internet users with many of the new CSS-related terms and jargon.

If there are any other CSS terms you would like added to this list, e-mail me at **rfalla@netroute.net** with the proposed term and its definition, and I will add it to the online version of this book—if it's appropriate.

Attribute   Many HTML and CSS1 properties have a list of attributes, or selectors. You can choose an appropriate attribute to make the property or element more specific.

Block Level Element   Block level elements are HTML elements that have a BR (line break) before and after the element. Images, headings, and <P> are examples of block level elements.

BODY   The body of the document is the area that is visible to the user through the aid of browser software. When defining the background of a document with CSS, BODY {background: [color] or [image (plus position)]} must be defined.

Browser   Also known as a client or UA, a browser is used to access the Internet and World Wide Web. Browsers, which are defined in SGML, read HTML, VRML, JavaScript, ActiveX, and CSS to determine the proper layout for the page. (See also *UA*.)

Canvas   The canvas is the area in the browser where the document is displayed. It is possible that the BODY of the HTML document and the canvas (CSS properties and attributes) will not match. If this happens, the visual part of the document that is included in the background of the canvas will not match the background of the HTML BODY. You can take advantage of that feature to create some interesting effects.

One way to avoid different backgrounds is to define the <BODY BGCOLOR="#*******"> (same as CSS background) in the head of the HTML document.

Classification Properties   These are CSS properties that categorize the elements rather than set specific visual parameters.

Contextual Selector

Contextual Selector   A contextual selector sets a list of simple selectors—HTML elements—as the basis for a conditional statement. The last simple selector is always the element addressed.

CSS   Cascading Style Sheets.

CSS1   Cascading Style Sheets Level 1, the specifications for using Cascading Style Sheets with the Web.

Declaration   A declaration consists of a CSS property and a legal value for that property.

Designer   The author of a CSS style sheet or an HTML Web site.

Document   An HTML document

Element   A distinctive component of an HTML document's structure, such as a title, heading, or list.

Extension   Additions to HTML are one way that commercial browser companies improve their products. Up to this point, browser companies have first added the new extensions to their own browser before attempting to get the extensions added to the HTML standards at the next Standards committee meeting.

Fictional Tag Sequence   Pseudo-classes and pseudo-elements are fictional tag sequences.

Floating Elements   Elements can be made to float over a document. If you set the properties of an image to `float:left`, the text will wrap around the right of the image.

Font-Encoding Fonts are assumed to come with a table that maps the font. The table also defines the size of that font.

Font-Matching   Browsers that are CSS1-compatible contain a database of fonts. The browser looks in the style sheet for font information when displaying a Web site. It first finds the font data on the style sheet and then matches the font to a font in the database.

If there are no fonts available in the database that match the specifications defined in the style sheet, the browser displays the default font in a best-match scenario.

Forms   Forms enable an audience to participate in a site. A site with a form is interactive.

Headers   With e-mail, the definition of header is quite simple. The header contains information about the message: to whom it is addressed, the author, and the message route from the sender to the receiver.

Height of Lines   All elements, except replaced elements, have a line height element. The total of the highest element on the line added to the leading equals the height of the line.

Homepage   The homepage is the front page of a Web site (the default URL) and is often used as an introductory page for the site.

Horizontal Formatting   The seven properties that influence the horizontal dimensions of the canvas and the boxes within the canvas are `margin-left`, `border-left`, `padding-left`, `width`, `padding-right`, `border-right`, and `margin-right`. The browser will set one of the margins to auto if the total of the values doesn't add up properly.

HTML   Hypertext Markup Language, the primary Internet presentation language.

HTML Extension   Additions to the language standard that are added by the commercial browsers to increase extensibility of HTML.

HTMLNOTE   A powerful HTML editor. This program is available as shareware for evaluation from Cranial Software. (**http://www.cranial.com/**)

HTTP   Hypertext Transport Protocol.

HWG (HTML Writers Guild)   This guild boasts a worldwide membership of almost 20,000 Internet professionals and hobbyists and can be found on the Internet at **www.hwg.org.**

Hyperlinks   Hyperlinks provide the user with a clickable link to another page on the same site or to an entirely different site. Both text and graphics can be hyperlinked.

Hypertext   The name of the text family that provides for hyperlinking of documents.

IMG   An HTML element or tag that instructs the browser where to place an image in the document. The source of the image is pointed to by using the `SRC=` element.

Initial

Initial   The default value of a CSS property.

Inline Element   An inline element is a non-blocklevel element.

Interactive   An Internet site is interactive if it allows users to affect the presentation by giving them a means of participating in the Web site, i.e., forms.

Intrinsic Dimension   The intrinsic dimensions are defined by the element and not by other external properties.

Keyword   Most CSS properties have keywords that may be used to further define the property.

Length Values   The length value is the value given to the length unit properties.

Level of Control   The level of control is determined by the weight given the command. With an author's `!important`, the level of control is tantamount to a dictatorship. The property cannot be overridden, even with a reader level of `!important`.

Links   Click a link to move to another page or site.

Lists   A list is an HTML listing that is marked with either a bullet (see options available with list-style) or a number.

MSIE (Microsoft Internet Explorer)   The first commercial Web browser to include CSS standards.

Multiple Pseudo-Elements   This is a listing of pseudo-elements, all of which are affected by the selector.

Netscape   Producers of the popular Web browser Netscape Navigator.

Property   HTML element modifiers that are available through CSS.

Pseudo-Class   Used to differentiate between element types.

Pseudo-Element   Used to address sub-parts of elements.

Pseudo-Elements in Selectors   These elements can be combined with CSS selectors, including contextual selectors. In the case of contextual selectors, only the last item, the addressed selector, can be a pseudo-element.

Relative Size   In CSS, this means relative to the size of the parent element.

Replaced Elements Images are replaced elements. The tag IMG is replaced by the data found at the URL pointed to in the SRC=.

Rule Rules consist of declarations and selectors.

Selector Defines the elements of the rule. There are two kinds of selectors: simple selectors and contextual selectors.

SGML (Standard General Markup Language) HTML is a child language to SGML. Web page elements HEAD and BODY are SGML elements.

Simple Selector CSS simple selectors are made up of HTML elements that are formatted according to properties in the declaration.

Site A group of related Web pages constitute a Web site.

SSI (Server-Side Include) An SSI command directs the server to run a program. An example of an SSI is an online form that sends a page to the user's browser, showing the data submitted.

Style Sheet A document that contains style information for formatting and displaying an HTML document.

Syntax A statement that contains pointers for the browser to display the page in a particular way.

Tag A slang reference to an HTML element.

Typographical Pseudo-Elements The first-line and first-letter elements in CSS.

UA (User Agent) Also known as a client or browser, a UA is used to access the Internet's World Wide Web. UA, defined in SGML, reads HTML and CSS to determine the proper layout for the page. See also *browser*.

Units A way to express length properties in known units.

URL A Uniform Resource Locator is used to specify the name and address of an Internet document.

Value A value is a number.

Vertical Formatting Vertical Formatting causes collapsing margins to properly display the canvas area.

W3C (World Wide Web Consortium)

W3C (World Wide Web Consortium)   The W3C makes the Standards for HTML CSS and other Internet technologies. The consortium is made up of institutional and corporate partners (members). If you are interested in learning more about the W3C, visit their Web site at **http://www.w3.org/**.

Weight   In CSS, weight refers to the priority of a declaration. Choices are `normal` and `!important`. For a user-defined style sheet to override the styles set by the document, the user must use `!important`. If the author of the document includes `!important`, the user cannot override the style.

INDEX

block level elements

Check out Que® Books
on the World Wide Web
http://www.mcp.com/que

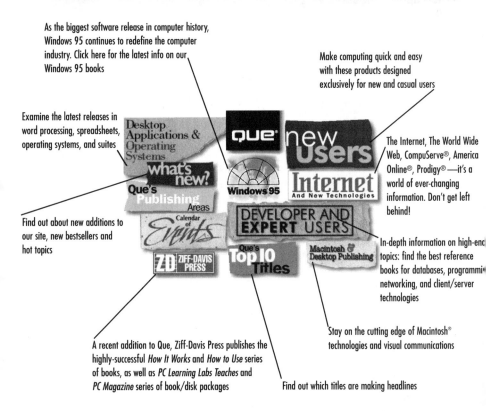

As the biggest software release in computer history, Windows 95 continues to redefine the computer industry. Click here for the latest info on our Windows 95 books

Make computing quick and easy with these products designed exclusively for new and casual users

Examine the latest releases in word processing, spreadsheets, operating systems, and suites

The Internet, The World Wide Web, CompuServe®, America Online®, Prodigy® —it's a world of ever-changing information. Don't get left behind!

Find out about new additions to our site, new bestsellers and hot topics

In-depth information on high-end topics: find the best reference books for databases, programming, networking, and client/server technologies

A recent addition to Que, Ziff-Davis Press publishes the highly-successful *How It Works* and *How to Use* series of books, as well as *PC Learning Labs Teaches* and *PC Magazine* series of book/disk packages

Stay on the cutting edge of Macintosh® technologies and visual communications

Find out which titles are making headlines

With 6 separate publishing groups, Que develops products for many specific market segments and areas of computer technology. Explore our Web Site and you'll find information on best-selling titles, newly published titles, upcoming products, authors, and much more.

- Stay informed on the latest industry trends and products available
- Visit our online bookstore for the latest information and editions
- Download software from Que's library of the best shareware and freeware

Complete and Return this Card
for a *FREE* Computer Book Catalog

Thank you for purchasing this book! You have purchased a superior computer book written expressly for your needs. To continue to provide the kind of up-to-date, pertinent coverage you've come to expect from us, we need to hear from you. Please take a minute to complete and return this self-addressed, postage-paid form. In return, we'll send you a free catalog of all our computer books on topics ranging from word processing to programming and the internet.

Mrs. ☐   Ms. ☐   Dr. ☐

(first) ☐   (M.I.) ☐ (last) ☐

ss ☐

State ☐   Zip ☐

Fax ☐

...ny Name ☐

... address ☐

Please check at least (3) influencing factors for purchasing this book.

...or back cover information on book .... ☐
...al approach to the content .... ☐
...leteness of content .... ☐
...r's reputation .... ☐
...her's reputation .... ☐
...cover design or layout .... ☐
...or table of contents of book .... ☐
...of book .... ☐
...l effects, graphics, illustrations .... ☐
...(Please specify): _____ ☐

How did you first learn about this book?

...t Site .... ☐
... Macmillan Computer
...lishing catalog .... ☐
...mended by store personnel .... ☐
...e book on bookshelf at store .... ☐
...mended by a friend .... ☐
...ved advertisement in the mail .... ☐
...n advertisement in: _____ ☐
...ook review in: _____ ☐
...(Please specify): _____ ☐

How many computer books have you purchased in the last six months?

...ook only .... ☐   3 to 5 books .... ☐
...s .... ☐   More than 5 .... ☐

4. Where did you purchase this book?

Bookstore .... ☐
Computer Store .... ☐
Consumer Electronics Store .... ☐
Department Store .... ☐
Office Club .... ☐
Warehouse Club .... ☐
Mail Order .... ☐
Direct from Publisher .... ☐
Internet site .... ☐
Other (Please specify): .... ☐

5. How long have you been using a computer?

Less than 6 months .. ☐   6 months to a year ..... ☐
1 to 3 years .... ☐   More than 3 years ...... ☐

6. What is your level of experience with personal computers and with the subject of this book?

	With PC's	With subject of book
New	☐	☐
Casual	☐	☐
Accomplished	☐	☐
Expert	☐	☐

Source Code — ISBN: 0-7897-1035-8

7. Which of the following best describes your job title?

Administrative Assistant .... ☐
Coordinator .... ☐
Manager/Supervisor .... ☐
Director .... ☐
Vice President .... ☐
President/CEO/COO .... ☐
Lawyer/Doctor/Medical Professional .... ☐
Teacher/Educator/Trainer .... ☐
Engineer/Technician .... ☐
Consultant .... ☐
Not employed/Student/Retired .... ☐
Other (Please specify): .... ☐

8. Which of the following best describes the area of the company your job title falls under?

Accounting .... ☐
Engineering .... ☐
Manufacturing .... ☐
Marketing .... ☐
Operations .... ☐
Sales .... ☐
Other (Please specify): .... ☐

9. What is your age?

Under 20 .... ☐
21-29 .... ☐
30-39 .... ☐
40-49 .... ☐
50-59 .... ☐
60-over .... ☐

10. Are you:

Male .... ☐
Female .... ☐

11. Which computer publications do you read regularly? (Please list)

_____
_____
_____
_____
_____
_____
_____
_____
_____
_____
_____

Comments: _____
_____
_____
_____

Fold here and scotch-tape to mail.